THE
SONG OF ROLAND

THE SONG OF ROLAND

DONE INTO ENGLISH IN THE ORIGINAL MEASURE BY

CHARLES SCOTT MONCRIEFF

WITH AN INTRODUCTION BY HAMISH MILES

ILLUSTRATED & HAND-ILLUMINATED BY VALENTI ANGELO

KALPAZ

ISBN: 978-93-5128-345-4(HB)

First Published in 1938
Indian Reprint in 2017

Published by

Kalpaz Publications
C-30, Satyawati Nagar,
Delhi – 110052
E-mail: kalpaz@hotmail.com
Website: kalpazpublications.com
Ph.: +91-9212142040

TO THREE MEN

SCHOLARS, POETS, SOLDIERS

WHO CAME TO THEIR RENCESVALS

IN SEPTEMBER, OCTOBER, AND NOVEMBER

NINETEEN HUNDRED AND EIGHTEEN

I DEDICATE MY PART

IN A BOOK

OF WHICH THEIR FRIENDSHIP

QUICKENED THE BEGINNING

THEIR EXAMPLE

HAS JUSTIFIED THE CONTINUING

∴

PHILIP BAINBRIGGE

WILFRED OWEN

IAN MACKENZIE

∴

"Mare fustes, seignurs.
Tutes voz anmes ait Deus li glorius.
En Parèis les metet en seintes flurs."

INTRODUCTION

I

ON the Spanish side of the Pyrenees, in the pass between St. Jean Pied de Port and Pamplona, lies the hamlet of Roncevaux—or, in its Spanish form, Roncesvalles. A narrow wooded valley, a cluster of humble dwellings, the quiet broken only by the water of a mountain stream edging its way southward into Navarre: there is nothing to show the casual eye that here is one of the great places of European legend, and that for over a thousand years its name has had in it the ring of battle and heroism, of poetry and grandeur. Or one thing only: the small chapel of the Holy Spirit near the stream. For by long tradition (and all this matter is one of tradition and legend more than of plain recorded history), that building marks the burial-place of Roland and the peers of Charlemagne who fell there, defeated, in battle against the Saracens in the year 778.

Il nen i ad ne veie ne senter,
Ne voide tere ne alne ne plein pied
Que il n'i ait o Franceis o paien . . .

There was no path nor passage anywhere,
Nor of waste ground no ell nor foot to spare
Without a Frank or pagan lying there . . .

And in the Bodleian Library at Oxford, in the strange quiet of rooms where the ardours and endeavours of men are preserved in writing for their posterity, lies the manuscript of the *Song of Roland*, which crystallised in poetry the memories and traditions of that day of disaster, of what went before it and came after it.

Many scholars in many countries have worked to discover the exact origins of the poem; how it grew; who wrote it in its full form and when; on what material this was based; which of its seven versions is the most sound; where historic fact ends and legend begins; and other such matters. But with these questions we need not here concern ourselves. We need only read the poem for its own sake, for its drama and character, and for its turbulent music, accepting (as modern scholarship does, especially since the labours of Joseph Bédier) the Oxford manuscript as the authoritative version. Its date may safely be placed in the twelfth century, perhaps four hundred years after the events which it commemorates. On that famous manuscript, in 1918-1919, Charles Scott Moncrieff based the verse translation here reprinted; and of the several English versions of the *Song of Roland* his stands out for its vigour and accuracy. "It is not," he wrote, "a work of scholarship, nor yet of imagination: it is an attempt to reproduce line for line, and, so far as is possible, word for word, the Old French epic poem." The spirit of the Pyrenean hills and of the warriors who fought their battles among them, passed many centuries ago into the four thousand lines of this epic. Scott Moncrieff, who himself knew hills and battles, and had mastered the tongue of the mediaeval poetry which celebrated them, was amply qualified to reconstruct this early masterpiece of French literature in an English equivalent. And his version richly deserves this revival.

II

To the modern eye the shape and pattern of the poem may seem confusing, almost rudimentary, rather as does that of a mediaeval painting or tapestry. But although the sequence of events, great and small, seems at first sight too swift and arbitrary, it is really compact, consecutive and satisfying. It may help the reader who is hearing the *Song of Roland* for the first time (and it is a poem for the ear rather than the eye) to describe the technical structure of the poem, and to sketch in bare outline the events which it describes.

The poem, then, consists of two hundred and ninety-one strophes, or *laisses*, of unequal length, each *laisse* obtaining its steady beat from its ten-syllabled lines and from the assonances at the end of each line. Here, for instance, is the opening *laisse*:

Carles li reis, nostre emperere magnes,
Set anz tuz pleins ad estet en Espaigne:
Tresqu'en la mer cunquist la tere altaigne.
N'i ad castel ki devant lui remaigne.
Mur ne citet n'i est remés a fraindre,
Fors Sarraguce, ki est en une muntaigne.
Le reis Marsilie la tient, ki Deu nen aimet.
Mahumet sert e Apollin recleimet:
Nes poet guarder que mals ne l'i ateignet. AOI.*

* Scholars disagree as to the significance of the exclamatory 'AOI' which recurs at the end of many of the *laisses*. But most readers will be satisfied to accept it as a kind of chanted refrain.

And a glance forward at the corresponding English strophe, the first, will show how Scott Moncrieff reproduces both the metrical rhythm and the assonance of the lines. The syntax throughout is of the simplest sort (far more so than, say, that of the Homeric poems): everything is told in short, direct, almost stiff sentences; but the cumulative effect of their simplicity is extremely powerful. It does not follow, however, that the poem is lacking in artistry, or that it should be viewed as a "crude" or "popular" versification. The *Song of Roland* is not in the class of the "popular" ballad or the penny-plain-twopence-coloured print: it is full of conscious artistry in its composition. As Joseph Bédier wrote in prefacing his great edition of the text, it has an aristocratic mien; its language is not only coloured with fine shades and deliberate subtlety, but "reveals a constant care to distinguish common usage from proper usage". The style indeed, as he says, is already that of a classic; it has its own nobility, a reflection of that sense of a national, aristocratic culture which was coming into flower in France during the twelfth century.

III

History lies beneath the rhythm and drama of this great *chanson de geste*; but the recorded facts of Charlemagne's deeds in Northern Spain at this time are sparse and fragmentary. In the epic they are obviously amplified by memories of earlier events, such as the expedition of Dagobert against the Basques in 636-637, wherein Harembert and other Frankish chiefs were slain. But the Frankish Emperor certainly led an expedition down to the Christian city of Pamplona in the year 778, mastered several Saracen strongholds, and was checked at Saragossa. Heading northwards again, the rearguard of his army was ambushed, somewhere, by the lightly armed Basque mountaineers, and in the battle, according to Einhard's *Vita Caroli*, many of the Emperor's chieftains were slain: notably one Hrodland, Count of the Breton Marches. And in this Hrodland we catch sight of the man whom legend transformed into the heroic figure of Roland, and round whom gathered other figures of noble stature, such as his friend Oliver and the Archbishop Turpin of Rheims. Roncevaux itself is not vouched for by the historic chronicles as the scene of the battle; but the persistence of the tradition that here the disaster befell, and the geographical facts facing an army heading north from Pamplona, make it reasonably easy to accept Roncevaux as the true site.

But the *Song of Roland* has a richer tale to tell; and to summarise the poem, albeit barely, may help some readers to grasp more readily its shape, its unity, its scope.

The poem is continuous, but it falls into five main parts. In the first (*lines* 1–702), the stage is set and the chief persons of the drama set upon it. Charlemagne has for seven weary years been battling against the Saracens in Spain, and only the city of Saragossa, where the pagan King Marsile reigns, stands against him. When Marsile offers terms of peace, the Emperor summons his peers to consider them. Roland casts doubt on the pagan king's good faith, and urges war *à outrance*; but his father-in-law, Ganelon, with certain other lords of weight, counsels acceptance, and treacherously plots with Blancandrins, the pagan envoy, to avenge himself on Roland by so contriving the march of the Emperor's army that Roland shall be in the rearguard, which, when it enters the pass of Roncevaux, will be cut off and destroyed by the pagans. And as this scene closes—

. . . . a thousand trumpets blare.
Franks leave their lines; the sumpter beasts are yare;
T'wards France the Douce all on their way repair.

Then comes the second part (*lines* 703-1016). The army of Charlemagne is marching on its northward way, and Ganelon suggests that Roland shall be chosen to command the rearguard through the dangerous defiles. In his pride, Roland accepts and takes with him his trusty friend Oliver, amongst others of renown, and refuses the greater body of men which Charlemagne, feeling apprehensive, is willing to give him. And the fateful march goes on:

High are the peaks, the valleys shadowful,
Swarthy the rocks, the narrows wonderful.
Franks passed that day all very sorrowful.

And as they go, the pagans are planning the attack on Roland. He hears the distant clamour of their "thousand horns", but is undaunted:

"Now must we each lay on most hardily,
So evil songs ne'er sung of us shall be.
Pagans are wrong: Christians are right indeed.
Evil example will never come of me!"

And there, with the besetting Saracens pressing in on them from the hills, the third and greatest part of the *Song of Roland* begins (*lines* 1017-2396). The force of the pagans is overpowering, and Oliver would have Roland sound his horn that Charlemagne may hear and turn back to give them aid. Three times he exhorts Roland, but three times Roland refuses, unwilling to dishonour his name and fame. At first the battle turns in favour of the Franks, but things go ill with them, and few are left alive save Roland, Oliver and Turpin. At last, but now too late, Roland consents "to sound his oliphant with grief and pain". The Emperor recognises from afar that, if Roland gives forth this signal, it must be one of dire distress. Ganelon would fain prevent him from turning on his tracks, but Charlemagne marches back, after seeing that Ganelon is a traitor:

> "Guard me him well, his felony is plain,
> Who in my house vile treachery has made. . ."

But he is too late. At Roncevaux Oliver is dead; the Saracens take to flight at the sound of the Emperor's return, but on the stricken field the only survivors, Roland and Turpin, are dying men. Turpin dies first, after blessing the dead; Roland bids farewell to his good sword, Durendal by name, and tries in vain to break it on a rock. And then, with Durendal laid beneath him, and turning his face to the fleeing foe, Roland himself dies, holding up the glove of challenge to heaven.*

* The memory of the conflict is preserved on the pagan's side as well, in a different light. There survives a curious traditional song of the mountaineers of Altabizcar, the *Altabizcaren Cantua*, from which come these lines, which I render freely:

> *They come, they come!*
> *Child, count them well,*
> *One, two, three, four, five,*

These are the greatest scenes and the greatest glories of the poem. But the drama is not completed. In the fourth part (*lines* 2397-3704) the vengeance of Charlemagne on the pagans is described. He chases the Saracens even to the Ebro, and when Marsile seeks the aid of the Emir of Babylon, Baligant, the Emperor crushes this force too, and returns to his seat at Aix.

And there, in the final part of the poem (*lines* 3705-4002), the story is brought to a close. The Emperor receives the unhappy Alde, betrothed to Roland, who dies of grief when she learns that he is dead. He then summons a council to pass judgment on Ganelon, who "... wealth to gain betrayed the dozen peers". His kinsman Pinabel agrees to stand as his champion against Tierri, the avenger of the dead Roland. The combat ends with the slaying of Pinabel, and Ganelon

Six, seven, eight, nine, ten,
Eleven, twelve, thirteen, fourteen, fifteen,
Sixteen, seventeen, eighteen, nineteen, twenty!
Twenty, yea—and thousands beside.
But the rocks as they fall will crush the hosts.
Blood flows, the mangled flesh quivers.
Lo! All these crushed bones!
Lo! the great tide of blood.

They flee, they flee!
And where now is the hedge of lances?
How many are they?
Count them, child, count them well.
Twenty, nineteen, eighteen, seventeen, sixteen,
Fifteen, fourteen, thirteen, twelve, eleven,
Ten, nine, eight, seven, six,
Five, four, three, two, one!
It is ended. . .
At dusk the eagles will swoop to tear that mangled flesh,
And those bones will lie there bleaching
For ever and a day!

in his turn has to die a traitor's cruel death, torn asunder by four stallions, "a felon recreant".

IV

So ends the Song. At the very last it strikes, as it were, an unresolved chord, almost as if it were prepared to tell and celebrate more. For in the concluding lines the aged Emperor, the soldier of God, is visited in a dream by the Archangel Gabriel, who calls upon him to embark on yet another war with paganism.

> "God," said the King. "My life is hard indeed!"
> Tears filled his eyes, he tore his snowy beard.

But no more is told, and with that the *Song of Roland* stands complete. And yet there is something deeply satisfying in the dying fall of that last strain, with its parting hint of fresh heroism in a new war against barbarism. "For that war," said G. K. Chesterton of these lines, when he introduced Scott Moncrieff's newly made translation, "is never ended, which defends the sanity of the world against all the stark anarchies and rending negations which rage against it for ever. That war is never finished in this world; and the grass has hardly grown on the graves of our own friends who fell in it." And truly its rumblings are still in our ears, however we may interpret the omens in the Eastern sky and the Western. So long as men may be called upon to do battle for what they hold to be the right, so long will the *Song of Roland* sound in their ears. For it is compact of verities that change not.

HAMISH MILES

THE SONG OF ROLAND

THE SONG OF ROLAND

I

Charlès the King, our Lord and Sovereign,
Full seven years hath sojournèd in Spain,
Conquered the land, and won the
western main.
Now no fortress against him doth remain,
No city walls are left for him to gain,
Save Sarraguce, that sits on high mountain.
Marsile its King, who feareth not God's name,
Mahumet's man, he invokes Apollin's aid,
Nor wards off ills that shall to him attain. AOI.

II

King Marsilies he lay at Sarraguce,
Went he his way into an orchard cool;
There on a throne he sate, of marble blue,
Round him his men, full twenty thousand, stood.
Called he forth then his counts, also his dukes:
"My Lords, give ear to our impending doom:
That Emperour, Charlès of France the Douce,
Into this land is come, us to confuse.
I have no host in battle him to prove,
Nor have I strength his forces to undo.
Counsel me then, ye that are wise and true;
Can ye ward off this present death and dule?"
What word to say, no pagan of them knew,
Save Blancandrins, of th' Castle of Val Funde.

III

Blancandrins was a pagan very wise;
In vassalage he was a gallant knight,
First in prowess, he stood his lord beside.
And thus he spoke: "Do not yourself affright!
Yield to Carlun, that is so big with pride,
Faithful service, his friend and his ally;
Lions and bears and hounds for him provide,
Thousand mewed hawks, sev'n hundred camelry;
Silver and gold, four hundred mules load high;
Fifty wagons his wrights will need supply,
Till with that wealth he pays his soldiery.
War hath he waged in Spain too long a time,
To Aix, in France, homeward he will him hie.
Follow him there before Saint Michael's tide,
You shall receive and hold the Christian rite;
Stand honour bound, and do him fealty.
Send hostages, should he demand surety,

Ten or a score, our loyal oath to bind;
Send him our sons, the first-born of our wives;—
An he be slain, I'll surely furnish mine.
Better by far they go, though doomed to die,
Than that we lose honour and dignity,
And be ourselves brought down to beggary." AOI.

IV

Says Blancandrins: "By my right hand, I say,
And by this beard that in the wind doth sway,
The Frankish host you'll see them all away;
Franks will retire to France their own terrain.
When they are gone, to each his fair domain,
In his Chapelle at Aix will Charlès stay,
High festival will hold for Saint Michael.
Time will go by, and pass the appointed day;
Tidings of us no Frank will hear or say.
Proud is that King, and cruel his courage;
From th' hostages he'll slice their heads away.
Better by far their heads be shorn away,
Than that ourselves lose this clear land of Spain,
Than that ourselves do suffer grief and pain."
"Maybe he speaks good truth," the pagans say.

V

The council ends, and that King Marsilie
Calleth aside Clarun of Balaguee,
Estramarin and Eudropin his peer,
And Priamun and Guarlan of the beard,
And Machiner and his uncle Mahee,
With Joüner, Malbien from over sea,
And Blancandrins, good reason to decree:
Ten hath he called, were first in felony.
"Gentle Barons, to Charlemagne go ye;
He is in siege of Cordres the city.

In your right hands bear olive-branches green
Which signify Peace and Humility.
If you by craft contrive to set me free,
Silver and gold, you'll have your fill of me,
Manors and fiefs, I'll give you all your need."
"We have enough," the pagans straight agree.

VI

King Marsilies, his council finishing,
Says to his men: "Go now, my lords to him,
Olive-branches in your right hands bearing;
Bid ye for me this Charlemagne, the King,
In his God's name to shew me his mercy;
Ere this new moon wanes, I shall be with him;
One thousand men shall be my following;
I will receive the rite of christening,
Will be his man, my love and faith swearing;
Hostages too he'll have, if so he will."
Says Blancandrins: "Much good will come of this."
AOI.

VII

Ten snow-white mules then ordered Marsilie,
Gifts of a King, the King of Suatilie.
Bridled with gold, saddled in silver clear;
Mounted them those that should the message speak,
In their right hands were olive-branches green.
Came they to Charle, that holds all France in fee,
Yet cannot guard himself from treachery. AOI.

VIII

Merry and bold is now that Emperour,
Cordres he holds, the walls are tumbled down,
His catapults have battered town and tow'r.
Great good treasure his knights have placed in pound,
Silver and gold and many a jewelled gown.

In that city there is no pagan now
But he be slain, or takes the Christian vow.
The Emperour is in a great orchard ground
Where Oliver and Rollant stand around,
Sansun the Duke and Anséis the proud,
Gefreid d'Anjou, that bears his gonfaloun;
There too Gerin and Geriers are found.
Where they are found, is seen a mighty crowd,
Fifteen thousand, come out of France the Douce.
On white carpets those knights have sate them down,
At the game-boards to pass an idle hour—
Chequers the old, for wisdom most renowned,
While fence the young and lusty bachelours.
Beneath a pine, in eglantine embow'red,
Stands a fald-stool, fashioned of gold throughout;
There sits the King that holds Douce France in pow'r;
White is his beard, and blossoming-white his crown,
Shapely his limbs, his countenance is proud.
Should any seek, no need to point him out.
The messengers, on foot they got them down,
And in salute full courteously they lout.

IX

The foremost word of all Blancandrins spake,
And to the King: "May God preserve you safe,
The All Glorious, to Whom ye're bound to pray!
Proud Marsilies this message bids me say:
Much hath he sought to find salvation's way;
Out of his wealth meet presents would he make,
Lions and bears, and greyhounds leashed on chain,
Thousand mewed hawks, sev'n hundred dromedrays,
Four hundred mules his silver shall convey,
Fifty wagons you'll need to bear away
Golden besants, such store of proved assay,

Wherewith full tale your soldiers you can pay.
Now in this land you've been too long a day;
Hie you to France, return again to Aix:
Thus saith my Lord, he'll follow too that way."
That Emperour towards God his arms he raised
Lowered his head, began to meditate. AOI.

X

That Emperour inclined his head full low;
Hasty in speech he never was, but slow:
His custom was, at his leisure he spoke.
When he looks up, his face is very bold,
He says to them: "Good tidings have you told.
King Marsilies hath ever been my foe.
These very words you have before me told,
In what measure of faith am I to hold?"
That Sarrazin says, "Hostages he'll show;
Ten shall you take, or fifteen or a score.
Though he be slain, a son of mine shall go,
Any there be you'll have more nobly born.
To your palace seigneurial when you go,
At Michael's Feast, called *in periculo*;
My Lord hath said, thither will he follow
Ev'n to your baths, that God for you hath wrought;
There is he fain the Christian faith to know."
Answers him Charles: "Still may he heal his soul."
AOI.

XI

Clear shone the sun in a fair even-tide;
Those ten men's mules in stall he bade them tie.
Also a tent in the orchard raise on high,
Those messengers had lodging for the night;
Dozen serjeants served after them aright.
Darkling they lie till comes the clear daylight.

That Emperour does with the morning rise;
Matins and Mass are said then in his sight.
Forth goes that King, and stays beneath a pine;
Barons he calls, good counsel to define,
For with his Franks he's ever of a mind. AOI.

XII

That Emperour, beneath a pine he sits,
Calls his barons, his council to begin:
Oger the Duke, that Archbishop Turpin,
Richard the old, and his nephew Henry,
From Gascony the proof Count Acolin,
Tedbald of Reims and Milun his cousin:
With him there were Gerers, also Gerin,
And among them the Count Rollant came in,
And Oliver, so proof and so gentil.
Franks out of France, a thousand chivalry;
Guenès came there, that wrought the treachery.
The Council then began, which ended ill. AOI.

XIII

"My Lord Barons," says the Emperour then, Charlès,
"King Marsilies hath sent me his messages;
Out of his wealth he'll give me weighty masses.
Greyhounds on leash and bears and lions also,
Thousand mewed hawks and seven hundred camels,
Four hundred mules with gold Arabian chargèd,
Fifty wagons, yea more than fifty drawing.
But into France demands he my departure;
He'll follow me to Aix, where is my Castle;
There he'll receive the law of our Salvation:
Christian he'll be, and hold from me his marches.
But I know not what purpose in his heart is."
Then say the Franks: "Beseems us act with caution!"
AOI.

XIV

That Emperour hath ended now his speech.
The Count Rollant, he never will agree;
Quick to reply, he springs upon his feet,
And to the King, "Believe not Marsilie.
Seven years since, when into Spain came we,
I conquer'd you Noples also Commibles,
And took Valterne, and all the land of Pine,
And Balaguet, and Tuele, and Sezilie.
Traitor in all his ways was Marsilies;
Of his pagans he sent you then fifteen,
Bearing in hand their olive-branches green;
Who, ev'n as now, these very words did speak.
You of your Franks a Council did decree,
Praised they your words that foolish were in deed.
Two of your Counts did to the pagan speed,
Basan was one, and the other Basilie:
Their heads he took on th' hill by Haltilie.
War have you waged, so on to war proceed,
To Sarraguce lead forth your great army.
All your life long, if need be, lie in siege,
Vengeance for those the felon slew to wreak." AOI.

XV

That Emperour he sits with lowering front,
He clasps his chin, his beard his fingers tug,
Good word nor bad, his nephew hears not one.
Franks hold their peace, but only Guenelun
Springs to his feet, and comes before Carlun;
Right haughtily his reason he's begun,
And to the King: "Believe not any one,
My word nor theirs, save whence your good shall come.
Since he sends word, that King Marsiliun,
Homage he'll do, by finger and by thumb;

Throughout all Spain your writ alone shall run;
Next he'll receive our rule of Christendom;
Who shall advise, this bidding be not done,
Deserves not death, since all to death must come.
Counsel of pride is wrong: we've fought enough.
Leave we the fools, and with the wise be one." AOI.

XVI

And after him came Neimès out, the third,
Better vassal there was not in the world;
And to the King; "Now rightly have you heard
Guenès the Count, what answer he returned.
Wisdom was there, but let it well be heard.
King Marsilies in war is overturned,
His castles all in ruin have you hurled,
With catapults his ramparts have you burst,
Vanquished his men, and all his cities burned;
Him who entreats your pity do not spurn,
Sinners were they that would to war return;
With hostages his faith he would secure;
Let this great war no longer now endure."
"Well spake the Duke," Franks utter in their turn. AOI.

XVII

"My lords barons, say whom shall we send up
To Sarraguce, to King Marsiliun?"
Answers Duke Neimes: "I'll go there for your love;
Give me therefore the wand, also the glove."
Answers the King: "Old man of wisdom pruff;
By this white beard, and as these cheeks are rough,
You'll not this year so far from me remove;
Go sit you down, for none hath called you up."

XVIII

"My lords barons, say whom now can we send
To th' Sarrazin that Sarraguce defends?"

Answers Rollant: "I might go very well."
"Certes, you'll not," says Oliver his friend,
"For your courage is fierce unto the end,
I am afraid you would misapprehend.
If the King wills it I might go there well."
Answers the King: "Be silent both on bench;
Your feet nor his, I say, shall that way wend.
Nay, by this beard, that you have seen grow blench,
The dozen peers by that would stand condemned.
Franks hold their peace; you'd seen them all silent."

XIX

Turpin of Reims is risen from his rank,
Says to the King: "In peace now leave your Franks.
For seven years you've lingered in this land;
They have endured much pain and sufferance.
Give, Sire, to me the glove, also the wand,
I will seek out the Spanish Sarazand,
For I believe his thoughts I understand."
That Emperour answers intolerant:
"Go, sit you down on yonder silken mat;
And speak no more until that I command." AOI.

XX

"Franks, chevaliers," says the Emperour then, Charlès,
"Choose ye me out a baron from my marches,
To Marsilie shall carry back my answer."
Then says Rollant: "There's Guenès, my good-father."
Answer the Franks: "For he can wisely manage;
So let him go, there's none you should send rather."
And that count Guenes is very full of anguish;
Off from his neck he flings the pelts of marten,
And on his feet stands clear in silken garment.
Proud face he had, his eyes with colour sparkled;
Fine limbs he had, his ribs were broadly archèd;

So fair he seemed that all the court regarded.
Says to Rollant: "Fool, wherefore art so wrathful?
All men know well that I am thy good-father;
Thou hast decreed, to Marsiliun I travel.
Then if God grant that I return hereafter,
I'll follow thee with such a force of passion
That will endure so long as life may last thee."
Answers Rollant: "Thou'rt full of pride and madness.
All men know well, I take no thought for slander;
But some wise man, surely, should bear the answer;
If the King will, I'm ready to go rather." AOI.

XXI

Answers him Guene: "Thou shalt not go for me.
Thou'rt not my man, nor am I lord of thee.
Charlès commands that I do his decree,
To Sarraguce going to Marsilie;
There I will work a little trickery,
This mighty wrath of mine I'll thus let free."
When Rollant heard, began to laugh for glee. AOI.

XXII

When Guenès sees that Rollant laughs at it,
Such grief he has, for rage he's like to split,
A little more, and he has lost his wit:
Says to that count: "I love you not a bit;
A false judgement you bore me when you chid.
Right Emperour, you see me where you sit,
I will your word accomplish, as you bid. AOI.

XXIII

"To Sarraguce I must repair, 'tis plain;
Whence who goes there returns no more again.
Your sister's hand in marriage have I ta'en;
And I've a son, there is no prettier swain:
Baldwin, men say he shews the knightly strain.

To him I leave my honours and domain.
Care well for him; he'll look for me in vain."
Answers him Charles: "Your heart is too humane.
When I command, time is to start amain." AOI.

XXIV

Then says the King: "Guenès, before me stand;
And take from me the glove, also the wand.
For you have heard, you're chosen by the Franks."
"Sire," answers Guenes, "all this is from Rollant;
I'll not love him, so long as I'm a man,
Nor Oliver, who goes at his right hand;
The dozen peers, for they are of his band,
All I defy, as in your sight I stand."
Then says the King: "Over intolerant,
Now certainly you go when I command."
"And go I can; yet have I no warrant;
Basile had none nor his brother Basant."

XXV

His right-hand glove that Emperour holds out;
But the count Guenes elsewhere would fain be found;
When he should take, it falls upon the ground.
Murmur the Franks: "God! What may that mean now?
By this message great loss shall come about."
"Lordings," says Guene, "you'll soon have news enow."

XXVI

"Now," Guenès said, "give me your orders, Sire;
Since I must go, why need I linger, I?"
Then said the King: "In Jesu's Name and mine!"
With his right hand he has absolved and signed,
Then to his care the wand and brief confides.

XXVII

Guenès the count goes to his hostelry,
Finds for the road his garments and his gear,

All of the best he takes that may appear:
Spurs of fine gold he fastens on his feet,
And to his side Murglès his sword of steel.
On Tachebrun, his charger, next he leaps,
His uncle holds the stirrup, Guinemere.
Then you had seen so many knights to weep,
Who all exclaim: "Unlucky lord, indeed!
In the King's court these many years you've been,
Noble vassal, they say that have you seen.
He that for you this journey has decreed,
King Charlemagne will never hold him dear.
The Count Rollant, he should not so have deemed,
Knowing you were born of very noble breed."
After they say: "Us too, Sire, shall he lead."
Then answers Guenes: "Not so, the Lord be pleased!
Far better one than many knights should bleed.
To France the Douce, my lords, you soon shall speed,
On my behalf my gentle wife you'll greet,
And Pinabel, who is my friend and peer,
And Baldëwin, my son, whom you have seen;
His rights accord and help him in his need."
—Rides down the road, and on his way goes he.
AOI.

XXVIII

Guenes canters on, and halts beneath a tree;
Where Sarrazins assembled he may see,
With Blancandrins, who abides his company.
Cunning and keen they speak then, each to each,
Says Blancandrins; "Charles, what a man is he,
Who conquered Puille and th' whole of Calabrie;
Into England he crossed the bitter sea,
To th' holy Pope restored again his fee.
What seeks he now of us in our country?"

Then answers Guene: "So great courage hath he;
Never was man against him might succeed." AOI.

XXIX

Says Blancandrins: "Gentle the Franks are found;
Yet a great wrong these dukes do and these counts
Unto their lord, being in counsel proud;
Him and themselves they harry and confound."
Guenes replies: "There is none such, without
Only Rollant, whom shame will yet find out.
Once in the shade the King had sate him down;
His nephew came, in sark of iron brown,
Spoils he had won, beyond by Carcasoune,
Held in his hand an apple red and round.
"Behold, fair Sire," said Rollant as he bowed,
"Of all earth's kings I bring you here the crowns."
His cruel pride must shortly him confound,
Each day t'wards death he goes a little down,
When he be slain, shall peace once more abound." AOI.

XXX

Says Blancandrins: "A cruel man, Rollant,
That would bring down to bondage every man,
And challenges the peace of every land.
With what people takes he this task in hand?"
And answers Guene: "The people of the Franks;
They love him so, for men he'll never want.
Silver and gold he show'rs upon his band,
Chargers and mules, garments and silken mats.
The King himself holds all by his command;
From hence to the East he'll conquer sea and land."

XXXI AOI.

Cantered so far then Blancandrins and Guene
Till each by each a covenant had made
And sought a plan, how Rollant might be slain.

Cantered so far by valley and by plain
To Sarraguce beneath a cliff they came.
There a fald-stool stood in a pine-tree's shade,
Enveloped all in Alexandrin veils;
There was the King that held the whole of Espain,
Twenty thousand of Sarrazins his train;
Nor was there one but did his speech contain,
Eager for news, till they might hear the tale.
Haste into sight then Blancandrins and Guene.

XXXII

Blancandrins comes before Marsiliun,
Holding the hand of county Guenelun;
Says to the King: "Lord save you, Sire, Mahum
And Apollin, whose holy laws here run!
Your message we delivered to Charlun,
Both his two hands he raised against the sun,
Praising his God, but answer made he none.
He sends you here his noblest born barun,
Greatest in wealth, that out of France is come;
From him you'll hear if peace shall be, or none."
"Speak," said Marsile: "We'll hear him, every one."
AOI.

XXXIII

But the count Guenes did deeply meditate;
Cunning and keen began at length, and spake
Even as one that knoweth well the way;
And to the King: "May God preserve you safe,
The All Glorious, to whom we're bound to pray.
Proud Charlemagne this message bids me say:
You must receive the holy Christian Faith,
And yield in fee one half the lands of Spain.
If to accord this tribute you disdain,
Taken by force and bound in iron chain

You will be brought before his throne at Aix;
Judged and condemned you'll be, and shortly slain,
Yes, you will die in misery and shame."
King Marsilies was very sore afraid,
Snatching a dart, with golden feathers gay,
He made to strike: they turned aside his aim. AOI.

XXXIV

King Marsilies is turnèd white with rage,
His feathered dart he brandishes and shakes.
Guenes beholds: his sword in hand he takes,
Two fingers' width from scabbard bares the blade;
And says to it: "O clear and fair and brave;
Before this King in court we'll so behave,
That the Emperour of France shall never say
In a strange land I'd thrown my life away
Before these chiefs thy temper had essayed."
"Let us prevent this fight," the pagans say.

XXXV

Then Sarrazins implored him so, the chiefs,
On the fald-stool Marsilies took his seat.
"Greatly you harm our cause," says the alcaliph:
"When on this Frank your vengeance you would wreak;
Rather you should listen to hear him speak."
"Sire," Guenès says, "to suffer I am meek.
I will not fail, for all the gold God keeps,
Nay, should this land its treasures pile in heaps,
But I will tell, so long as I be free,
What Charlemagne, that Royal Majesty,
Bids me inform his mortal enemy."
Guenès had on a cloke of sable skin,
And over it a veil Alexandrin;
These he throws down, they're held by Blancandrins;
But not his sword, he'll not leave hold of it,

In his right hand he grasps the golden hilt.
The pagans say: "A noble baron, this." AOI.

XXXVI

Before the King's face Guenès drawing near
Says to him: "Sire, wherefore this rage and fear?
Seeing you are, by Charles, of Franks the chief,
Bidden to hold the Christians' right belief.
One half of Spain he'll render as your fief,
The rest Rollant, his nephew, shall receive,
Proud parcener in him you'll have indeed.
If you will not to Charles this tribute cede,
To you he'll come, and Sarraguce besiege;
Take you by force, and bind you hands and feet,
Bear you outright e'en unto Aix his seat.
You will not then on palfrey nor on steed,
Jennet nor mule, come cantering in your speed;
Flung you will be on a vile sumpter-beast;
Tried there and judged, your head you will not keep.
Our Emperour has sent you here this brief."
He's given it into the pagan's nief.

XXXVII

Now Marsilies is turnèd white with ire,
He breaks the seal and casts the wax aside,
Looks in the brief, sees what the King did write:
"Charlès commands, who holds all France by might,
I bear in mind his bitter grief and ire;
'Tis of Basan and 's brother Basilye,
Whose heads I took on th' hill by Haltilye.
If I would save my body now alive,
I must despatch my uncle the alcaliph,
Charles will not love me ever otherwise."
After, there speaks his son to Marsilye,
Says to the King: "In madness spoke this wight.

So wrong he was, to spare him were not right;
Leave him to me, I will that wrong requite."
When Guenès hears, he draws his sword outright,
Against the trunk he stands, beneath that pine.

XXXVIII

The King is gone into that orchard then;
With him he takes the best among his men;
And Blancandrins there shews his snowy hair,
And Jursalet, was the King's son and heir,
And the alcaliph, his uncle and his friend.
Saith Blancandrins: "Summon the Frank again,
In our service his faith to me he's pledged."
Then says the King: "So let him now be fetched."
He's taken Guenes by his right finger-ends,
And through the orchard straight to the King they wend.
Of treason there make lawless parliament. AOI.

XXXIX

"Fair Master Guenes," says then King Marsilie,
"I did you now a little trickery,
Making to strike, I shewed my great fury.
These sable skins take as amends from me,
Five hundred pounds would not their worth redeem.
To-morrow night the gift shall ready be."
Guene answers him: "I'll not refuse it, me.
May God be pleased to show you His mercy." AOI.

XL

Then says Marsile: "Guenès, the truth to ken,
Minded I am to love you very well.
Of Charlemagne I wish to hear you tell,
He's very old, his time is nearly spent,
Two hundred years he's lived now, as 'tis said.
Through many lands his armies he has led,
So many blows his buckled shield has shed,

And so rich kings he's brought to beg their bread;
What time from war will he draw back instead?"
And answers Guenes: "Not so was Charlès bred.
There is no man that sees and knows him well
But will proclaim the Emperour's hardihead.
Praise him as best I may, when all is said,
Remain untold, honour and goodness yet.
His great valour how can it be counted?
Him with such grace hath God illuminèd,
Better to die than leave his banneret.

XLI

The pagan says: "You make me marvel sore
At Charlemagne, who is so old and hoar;
Two hundred years, they say, he's lived and more.
So many lands he's led his armies o'er,
So many blows from spears and lances borne,
And so rich kings brought down to beg and sorn,
When will time come that he draws back from war?"
"Never," says Guenes, "so long as lives his nephew;
No such vassal goes neath the dome of heaven;
And proof also is Oliver his henchman;
The dozen peers, whom Charlès holds so precious,
These are his guards, with other thousands twenty.
Charles is secure, he holds no man in terror." AOI.

XLII

Says Sarrazin: "My wonder yet is grand
At Charlemagne, who hoary is and blanched.
Two hundred years and more, I understand,
He has gone forth and conquered many a land,
Such blows hath borne from many a trenchant lance,
Vanquished and slain of kings so rich a band,
When will time come that he from war draws back?"
"Never," says Guene, "so long as lives Rollant,

From hence to the East there is no such vassal;
And proof also, Oliver his comrade;
The dozen peers he cherishes at hand,
These are his guard, with twenty thousand Franks.
Charles is secure, he fears no living man." AOI.

XLIII

"Fair Master Guenes," says Marsilies the King,
"Such men are mine, fairer than tongue can sing,
Of knights I can four hundred thousand bring
So I may fight with Franks and with their King."
Answers him Guenes: "Not on this journeying!
Save of pagans a great loss suffering.
Leave you the fools, wise counsel following;
To the Emperour such wealth of treasure give
That every Frank at once is marvelling.
For twenty men that you shall now send in
To France the Douce he will repair, that King;
In the rereward will follow after him
Both his nephew, count Rollant, as I think,
And Oliver, that courteous paladin;
Dead are the counts, believe me if you will.
Charles will behold his great pride perishing,
For battle then he'll have no more the skill." AOI.

XLIV

"Fair Master Guene," says then King Marsilie,
Shew the device, how Rollant slain may be."
Answers him Guenes: "That will I soon make clear:
The King will cross by the good pass of Size,
A guard he'll set behind him, in the rear;
His nephew there, count Rollant, that rich peer,
And Oliver, in whom he well believes;
Twenty thousand Franks in their company.
Five score thousand pagans upon them lead,

Franks unawares in battle you shall meet,
Bruised and bled white the race of Franks shall be;
I do not say, but yours shall also bleed.
Battle again deliver, and with speed.
So, first or last, from Rollant you'll be freed.
You will have wrought a high chivalrous deed,
Nor all your life know war again, but peace. AOI.

XLV

"Could one achieve that Rollant's life was lost,
Charlè's right arm were from his body torn;
Though there remained his marvellous great host.
He'ld not again assemble in such force;
Terra Major would languish in repose."
Marsile has heard, he's kissed him on the throat;
Next he begins to undo his treasure-store. AOI.

XLVI

Said Marsilie—but now what more said they?—
"No faith in words by oath unbound I lay;
Swear me the death of Rollant on that day."
Then answered Guene: "So be it, as you say."
On the relics, are in his sword Murglès,
Treason he's sworn, forsworn his faith away. AOI.

XLVII

Was a fald-stool there, made of olifant.
A book thereon Marsilies bade them plant
In it their laws, Mahum's and Tervagant's.
He's sworn thereby, the Spanish Sarazand,
In the rereward if he shall find Rollant,
Battle to give, himself and all his band,
And verily he'll slay him if he can.
And answered Guenes: "So be it, as you command!"
AOI.

XLVIII

In haste there came a pagan, Valdabrun,
Warden had been to King Marsiliun,
Smiling and clear, he's said to Guenelun:
"Take now this sword, and better sword has none;
Into the hilt a thousand coins are run.
To you, fair sir, I offer it in love;
Give us your aid from Rollant the barun,
That in rereward against him we may come."
Guenès the count answers: "It shall be done."
Then, cheek and chin, kissed each the other one.

XLIX

After there came a pagan, Climorins,
Smiling and clear to Guenelun begins:
"Take now my helm, better is none than this;
But give us aid, on Rollant the marquis
By what device we may dishonour bring."
"It shall be done," Count Guenés answered him.
On mouth and cheek then each the other kissed. AOI.

L

In haste there came the Queen forth, Bramimound;
"I love you well, sir," said she to the count,
"For prize you dear my lord and all around;
Here for your wife I have two brooches found,
Amethysts and jacynths in golden mount;
More worth are they than all the wealth of Roum;
Your Emperour has none such, I'll be bound."
He's taken them, and in his hosen pouched. AOI.

LI

The King now calls Malduiz, that guards his treasure.
"Tribute for Charles, say, is it now made ready?"
He answers him: "Ay, Sire, for here is plenty:
Silver and gold on hundred camels seven,

And twenty men, the gentlest under heaven." AOI.

LII

Marsilie's arm Guene's shoulder doth enfold;
He's said to him: "You are both wise and bold.
Now, by the law that you most sacred hold,
Let not your heart in our behalf grow cold!
Out of my store I'll give you wealth untold,
Charging ten mules with fine Arabian gold;
I'll do the same for you, new year and old.
Take then the keys of this city so large,
This great tribute present you first to Charles,
Then get me placed Rollant in the rereward.
If him I find in valley or in pass,
Battle I'll give him that shall be the last."
Answers him Guenes: "My time is nearly past."
His charger mounts, and on his journey starts. AOI.

LIII

That Emperour draws near to his domain,
He is come down unto the city Gailne.
The Count Rollant had broken it and ta'en,
An hundred years its ruins shall remain.
Of Guenelun the King for news is fain,
And for tribute from the great land of Spain.
At dawn of day, just as the light grows plain,
Into their camp is come the county Guene. AOI.

LIV

In morning time is risen the Emperere,
Mattins and Mass he's heard, and made his prayer;
On the green grass before the tent his chair,
Where Rollant stood and that bold Oliver,
Neimès the Duke, and many others there.
Guenès arrived, the felon perjurer,
Begins to speak, with very cunning air,

Says to the King: "God keep you, Sire, I swear!
Of Sarraguce the keys to you I bear,
Tribute I bring you, very great and rare,
And twenty men; look after them with care.
Proud Marsilies bade me this word declare:
That alcaliph, his uncle, you must spare.
My own eyes saw four hundred thousand there,
In hauberks dressed, closed helms that gleamed in the air,
And golden hilts upon their swords they bare.
They followed him, right to the sea they'ld fare;
Marsile they left, that would their faith forswear,
For Christendom they've neither wish nor care.
But the fourth league they had not compassed, ere
Brake from the North tempest and storm in the air;
Then were they drowned, they will no more appear.
Were he alive, I should have brought him here.
The pagan king, in truth, Sire, bids you hear,
Ere you have seen one month pass of this year
He'll follow you to France, to your Empire,
He will accept the laws you hold and fear;
Joining his hands, will do you homage there,
Kingdom of Spain will hold as you declare."
Then says the King: "Now God be praised, I swear!
Well have you wrought, and rich reward shall wear."
Bids through the host a thousand trumpets blare.
Franks leave their lines; the sumpter-beasts are yare;
T'wards France the Douce all on their way repair.
AOI.

LV

Charlès the Great that land of Spain had wasted,
Her castles ta'en, her cities violated.
Then said the King, his war was now abated.
Towards Douce France that Emperour has hasted.
Upon a lance Rollant his ensign raisèd,
High on a cliff against the sky 'twas placèd;
The Franks in camp through all that country baited.
Cantered pagans, through those wide valleys racèd,
Hauberks they wore and sarks with iron plated,
Swords to their sides were girt, their helms were lacèd,
Lances made sharp, escutcheons newly painted:
There in the mists beyond the peaks remainèd,
The day of doom four hundred thousand waited.
God! what a grief. Franks know not what is fated. AOI.

LVI

Passes the day, the darkness is grown deep.
That Emperour, rich Charlès, lies asleep;
Dreams that he stands in the great pass of Size,
In his two hands his ashen spear he sees;
Guenès the count that spear from him doth seize,
Brandishes it and twists it with such ease,
That flown into the sky the flinders seem.
Charlès sleeps on nor wakens from his dream.

LVII

And after this another vision saw,
In France, at Aix, in his Chapelle once more,
That his right arm an evil bear did gnaw;
Out of Ardennes he saw a leopard stalk,
His body dear did savagely assault;
But then there dashed a harrier from the hall,
Leaping in the air he sped to Charlè's call,
First the right ear of that grim bear he caught,
And furiously the leopard next he fought.
Of battle great the Franks then seemed to talk,
Yet which might win they knew not, in his thought.
Charlès sleeps on, nor wakens he for aught. AOI.

LVIII

Passes the night and opens the clear day;
That Emperour canters in brave array,
Looks through the host often and everyway;
"My lords barons," at length doth Charlès say,
"Ye see the pass along these valleys strait,
Judge for me now, who shall in rereward wait."
"There's my good-son, Rollant," then answers Guenes,
"You've no baron whose valour is as great."
When the King hears, he looks upon him straight,
And says to him: "You devil incarnate;

Into your heart is come a mortal hate.
And who shall go before me in the gate?"
"Oger is here, of Denmark," answers Guenes;
"You've no baron were better in that place." AOI.

LIX

The count Rollant hath heard himself decreed;
Speaks then to Guenes by rule of courtesy:
"Good-father, Sir, I ought to hold you dear,
Since the rereward you have for me decreed.
Charlès the King will never lose by me,
As I know well, nor charger nor palfrey,
Jennet nor mule that canter can with speed,
Nor sumpter-horse will lose, nor any steed,
But my sword's point shall first exact their meed."
Answers him Guenes; "I know; 'tis true indeed." AOI.

LX

When Rollant heard that he should be rerewarden
Furiously he spoke to his good-father:
"Aha! culvert; begotten of a bastard.
Thinkest the glove will slip from me hereafter,
As then from thee the wand fell before Charlès?" AOI.

LXI

"Right Emperour," says the baron Rollant,
"Give me the bow you carry in your hand;
Ne'er in reproach, I know, will any man
Say that it fell and lay upon the land,
As Guenes let fall, when he received the wand."
That Emperour with lowered front doth stand,
He tugs his beard, his chin is in his hand;
Tears fill his eyes, he cannot them command.

LXII

And after that is come duke Neimès furth,
(Better vassal there was not upon earth)

Says to the King: "Right well now have you heard;
The count Rollant to bitter wrath is stirred,
For that on him the rereward is conferred;
No baron else have you, would do that work.
Give him the bow your hands have bent, at first;
Then find him men, his company are worth."
Gives it, the King, and Rollant bears it furth.

LXIII

That Emperour, Rollant then calleth he:
"Fair nephew mine, know this in verity;
Half of my host I leave you presently;
Retain you them; your safeguard this shall be."
Then says the count: "I will not have them, me!
Confound me God, if I fail in the deed!
Good valiant Franks, a thousand score I'll keep.
Go through the pass in all security,
While I'm alive there's no man you need fear." AOI.

LXIV

The count Rollant has mounted his charger.
Beside him came his comrade Oliver,
Also Gerins and the proud count Geriers,
And Otès came, and also Berengiers,
Old Ansèis, and Sansun too came there;
Gerart also of Rossillon the fierce,
And there is come the Gascon Engeliers.
"Now by my head I'll go!" the Archbishop swears,
"And I'm with you," says then the count Gualtiers,
"I'm Rollant's man, I may not leave him there."
A thousand score they choose of chevaliers. AOI.

LXV

Gualter del Hum he calls, that Count Rollant;
"A thousand Franks take, out of France our land;
Dispose them so, among ravines and crags,

That the Emperour lose not a single man."
Gualter replies: "I'll do as you command."
A thousand Franks, come out of France their land,
At Gualter's word they scour ravines and crags;
They'll not come down, howe'er the news be bad,
Ere from their sheaths swords seven hundred flash.
King Almaris, Belserne for kingdom had,
On the evil day he met them in combat. AOI.

LXVI

High are the peaks, the valleys shadowful,
Swarthy the rocks, the narrows wonderful.
Franks passed that day all very sorrowful,
Fifteen leagues round the rumour of them grew.
When they were come, and Terra Major knew,
Saw Gascony their land and their seigneur's,
Remembering their fiefs and their honours,
Their little maids, their gentle wives and true;
There was not one that shed not tears for rue.
Beyond the rest Charles was of anguish full,
In Spanish Pass he'd left his dear nephew;
Pity him seized; he could but weep for rue. AOI.

LXVII

The dozen peers are left behind in Spain,
Franks in their band a thousand score remain,
No fear have these, death hold they in disdain.
That Emperour goes into France apace;
Under his cloke he fain would hide his face.
Up to his side comes cantering Duke Neimes,
Says to the King: "What grief upon you weighs?"
Charles answers him: "He's wrong that question makes.
So great my grief I cannot but complain.
France is destroyed, by the device of Guene:
This night I saw, by an angel's vision plain,

Between my hands he brake my spear in twain;
Great fear I have, since Rollant must remain:
I've left him there, upon a border strange.
God! If he's lost, I'll not outlive that shame." AOI.

LXVIII

Charlès the great, he cannot but deplore.
And with him Franks an hundred thousand mourn,
Who for Rollant have marvellous remorse.
The felon Guenes had treacherously wrought;
From pagan king has had his rich reward,
Silver and gold, and veils and silken cloths,
Camels, lions, with many a mule and horse.
Barons from Spain King Marsilies hath called,
Counts and viscounts and dukes and almacours,
And the admirals, and cadets nobly born;
Within three days come hundred thousands four.
In Sarraguce they sound the drums of war;
Mahum they raise upon their highest tow'r,
Pagan is none, that does not him adore.
They canter then with great contention
Through Certeine land, valleys and mountains, on,
Till of the Franks they see the gonfalons,
Being in rereward those dozen companions;
They will not fail battle to do anon.

LXIX

Marsile's nephew is come before the band,
Riding a mule, he goads it with a wand,
Smiling and clear, his uncle's ear demands:
"Fair Lord and King, since, in your service, glad,
I have endured sorrow and sufferance,
Have fought in field, and victories have had.
Give me a fee: the right to smite Rollant!
I'll slay him clean with my good trenchant lance,

If Mahumet will be my sure warrant;
Spain I'll set free, deliver all her land
From Pass of Aspre even unto Durestant.
Charles will grow faint, and recreant the Franks;
There'll be no war while you're a living man."
Marsilie gives the glove into his hand. AOI.

LXX

Marsile's nephew, holding in hand the glove,
His uncle calls, with reason proud enough:
"Fair Lord and King, great gift from you I've won.
Choose now for me eleven more baruns,
So I may fight those dozen companions."
First before all there answers Falfarun;
—Brother he was to King Marsiliun—
"Fair sir nephew, go you and I at once
Then verily this battle shall be done;
The rereward of the great host of Carlun,
It is decreed we deal them now their doom." AOI.

LXXI

King Corsablis is come from the other part,
Barbarian, and steeped in evil art.
He's spoken then as fits a good vassal,
For all God's gold he would not seem coward.
Hastes into view Malprimis of Brigal,
Faster than a horse, upon his feet can dart,
Before Marsile he cries with all his heart:
"My body I will shew at Rencesvals;
Find I Rollant, I'll slay him without fault."

LXXII

An admiral is there of Balaguet;
Clear face and proud, and body nobly bred;
Since first he was upon his horse mounted,
His arms to bear has shewn great lustihead;

In vassalage he is well famousèd;
Christian were he, he'd shewn good baronhead.
Before Marsile aloud has he shouted:
"To Rencesvals my body shall be led;
Find I Rollant, then is he surely dead,
And Oliver, and all the other twelve;
Franks shall be slain in grief and wretchedness.
Charles the great is old now and doted,
Weary will be and make no war again;
Spain shall be ours, in peace and quietness."
King Marsilies has heard and thanks him well. AOI.

LXXIII

An almacour is there of Moriane,
More felon none in all the land of Spain.
Before Marsile his vaunting boast hath made:
"To Rencesvals my company I'll take,
A thousand score, with shields and lances brave.
Find I Rollant, with death I'll him acquaint;
Day shall not dawn but Charles will make his plaint."
AOI.

LXXIV

From the other part, Turgis of Turtelose,
He was a count, that city was his own;
Christians he would them massacre, every one.
Before Marsile among the rest is gone,
Says to the King: "Let not dismay be shewn!
Mahum's more worth than Saint Peter of Rome;
Serve we him well, then fame in field we'll own.
To Rencesvals, to meet Rollant I'll go,
From death he'll find his warranty in none.
See here my sword that is both good and long,
With Durendal I'll lay it well across;
Ye'll hear betimes to which the prize is gone.

Franks shall be slain, whom we descend upon,
Charlès the old will suffer grief and wrong,
No more on earth his crown will he put on."

LXXV

From the other part, Escremiz of Valtrenne,
A Sarrazin, that land was his as well.
Before Marsile he cries amid the press:
"To Rencesvals I go, pride to make less;
Find I Rollant, he'll not bear thence his head,
Nor Oliver that hath the others led,
The dozen peers condemnèd are to death;
Franks shall be slain, and France lie deserted.
Of good vassals will Charles be richly bled." AOI.

LXXVI

From the other part, a pagan Esturganz;
Estramariz also, was his comrade;
Felons were these, and traitors miscreant.
Then said Marsile: "My Lords, before me stand!
Into the pass ye'll go to Rencesvals,
Give me your aid, and thither lead my band."
They answer him: "Sire, even as you command.
We will assault Olivier and Rollant,
The dozen peers from death have no warrant;
For these our swords are trusty and trenchant,
In scalding blood we'll dye their blades scarlat.
Franks shall be slain, and Charlès be right sad.
Terra Major we'll give into your hand;
Come there, Sir King, truly you'll see all that;
Yea, the Emperour we'll give into your hand."

LXXVII

Running there came Margariz of Sibile,
Who holds the land by Cadiz, to the sea.
For his beauty the ladies hold him dear;

Who looks on him, with him her heart is pleased,
When she beholds, she can but smile for glee.
Was no pagan of such high chivalry.
Comes through the press, above them all cries he,
"Be not at all dismayed, King Marsilie!
To Rencesvals I go, and Rollant, he
Nor Oliver may scape alive from me;
The dozen peers are doomed to martyry.
See here the sword, whose hilt is gold indeed,
I got in gift from the admiral of Primes;
In scarlat blood I pledge it shall be steeped.
Franks shall be slain, and France abasèd be.
To Charles the old, with his great blossoming beard,
Day shall not dawn but brings him rage and grief,
Ere a year pass, all France we shall have seized,
Till we can lie in th' burgh of Saint Denise."
The pagan king has bowed his head down deep. AOI.

LXXVIII

From the other part, Chernublès of Muneigre.
Right to the ground his hair swept either way;
He for a jest would bear a heavier weight
Than four yoked mules, beneath their load that strain.
That land he had, God's curse on it was plain.
No sun shone there, nor grew there any grain,
No dew fell there, nor any shower of rain,
The very stones were black upon that plain;
And many say that devils there remain.
Says Chernublès: "My sword is in its place,
At Rencesvals scarlat I will it stain;
Find I Rollant the proud upon my way,
I'll fall on him, or trust me not again,
And Durendal I'll conquer with this blade;
Franks shall be slain, and France a desert made."

The dozen peers are, at his word, away,
Five score thousand of Sarrazins they take;
Who keenly press, and on to battle haste;
In a fir-wood their gear they ready make.

LXXIX

Ready they make hauberks Sarrazinese,
That folded are, the greater part, in three;
And they lace on good helms Sarragucese;
Gird on their swords of tried steel Viennese;
Fine shields they have, and spears Valentinese,
And white, blue, red, their ensigns take the breeze,
They've left their mules behind, and their palfreys,
Their chargers mount, and canter knee by knee.
Fair shines the sun, the day is bright and clear,
Light burns again from all their polished gear.
A thousand horns they sound, more proud to seem;
Great is the noise, the Franks its echo hear.
Says Oliver: "Companion, I believe,
Sarrazins now in battle must we meet."
Answers Rollant: "God grant us then the fee!
For our King's sake well must we quit us here;
Man for his lord should suffer great disease,
Most bitter cold endure, and burning heat,
His hair and skin should offer up at need.
Now must we each lay on most hardily,
So evil songs ne'er sung of us shall be.
Pagans are wrong: Christians are right indeed.
Evil example will never come of me." AOI.

LXXX

Oliver mounts upon a lofty peak,
Looks to his right along a valley green,
The pagan tribes approaching there
appear;
He calls Rollant, his companion, to see:
"What sound is this, come out of Spain, we hear,
What hauberks bright, what helmets these that gleam?
They'll smite our Franks with fury past belief,
He knew it, Guenes, the traitor and the thief,
Who chose us out before the King our chief."
Answers the count Rollant: "Olivier, cease.
That man is my good-father; hold thy peace."

LXXXI

Upon a peak is Oliver mounted,
Kingdom of Spain he sees before him spread,
And Sarrazins, so many gatherèd.
Their helmets gleam, with gold are jewellèd,
Also their shields, their hauberks orfreyèd,
Also their swords, ensigns on spears fixèd.
Rank beyond rank could not be numberèd,
So many there, no measure could he set.
In his own heart he's sore astonishèd,
Fast as he could, down from the peak hath sped,
Comes to the Franks, to them his tale hath said.

LXXXII

Says Oliver: "Pagans from there I saw;
Never on earth did any man see more.
Gainst us their shields an hundred thousand bore,
That lacèd helms and shining hauberks wore;
And, bolt upright, their bright brown spearheads shone.
Battle we'll have as never was before.
Lords of the Franks, God keep you in valour!
So hold your ground, we be not overborne!"
Then say the Franks: "Shame take him that goes off:
If we must die, then perish one and all." AOI.

LXXXIII

Says Oliver: "Pagans in force abound,
While of us Franks but very few I count;
Comrade Rollant, your horn I pray you sound!
If Charlès hear, he'll turn his armies round."
Answers Rollant: "A fool I should be found;
In France the Douce would perish my renown.
With Durendal I'll lay on thick and stout,
In blood the blade, to its golden hilt, I'll drown.
Felon pagans to th' pass shall not come down;

I pledge you now, to death they all are bound." AOI.

LXXXIV

"Comrade Rollant, sound the olifant, I pray;
If Charlès hear, the host he'll turn again;
Will succour us our King and baronage."
Answers Rollant: "Never, by God, I say,
For my misdeed shall kinsmen hear the blame,
Nor France the Douce fall into evil fame!
Rather stout blows with Durendal I'll lay,
With my good sword that by my side doth sway;
Till bloodied o'er you shall behold the blade.
Felon pagans are gathered to their shame;
I pledge you now, to death they're doomed today."

LXXXV

"Comrade Rollant, once sound your olifant!
If Charlès hear, where in the pass he stands,
I pledge you now, they'll turn again, the Franks."
"Never, by God," then answers him Rollant,
"Shall it be said by any living man,
That for pagans I took my horn in hand!
Never by me shall men reproach my clan.
When I am come into the battle grand,
And blows lay on, by hundred, by thousand,
Of Durendal bloodied you'll see the brand.
Franks are good men; like vassals brave they'll stand;
Nay, Spanish men from death have no warrant."

LXXXVI

Says Oliver: "In this I see no blame;
I have beheld the Sarrazins of Spain;
Covered with them, the mountains and the vales,
The wastes I saw, and all the farthest plains.
A muster great they've made, this people strange;
We have of men a very little tale."

Answers Rollant: "My anger is inflamed.
Never, please God His Angels and His Saints,
Never by me shall Frankish valour fail!
Rather I'll die than shame shall me attain.
Therefore strike on, the Emperour's love to gain."

LXXXVII

Pride hath Rollant, wisdom Olivier hath;
And both of them shew marvellous courage;
Once they are horsed, once they have donned their arms,
Rather they'ld die than from the battle pass.
Good are the counts, and lofty their language.
Felon pagans come cantering in their wrath.
Says Oliver: "Behold and see, Rollant,
These are right near, but Charles is very far.
On the olifant deign now to sound a blast;
Were the King here, we should not fear damage.
Only look up towards the Pass of Aspre,
In sorrow there you'll see the whole rereward.
Who does this deed, does no more afterward."
Answers Rollant: "Utter not such outrage!
Evil his heart that is in thought coward!
We shall remain firm in our place installed;
From us the blows shall come, from us the assault."
AOI.

LXXXVIII

When Rollant sees that now must be combat,
More fierce he's found than lion or leopard;
The Franks he calls, and Oliver commands:
"Now say no more, my friends, nor thou, comrade.
That Emperour, who left us Franks on guard,
A thousand score stout men he set apart,
And well he knows, not one will prove coward.
Man for his lord should suffer with good heart,
Of bitter cold and great heat bear the smart,

His blood let drain, and all his flesh be scarred.
Strike with thy lance, and I with Durendal,
With my good sword that was the King's reward.
So, if I die, who has it afterward
Noble vassal's he well may say it was."

LXXXIX

From the other part is the Archbishop Turpin,
He pricks his horse and mounts upon a hill;
Calling the Franks, sermon to them begins:
"My lords barons, Charles left us here for this;
He is our King, well may we die for him:
To Christendom good service offering.
Battle you'll have, you all are bound to it,
For with your eyes you see the Sarrazins.
Pray for God's grace, confessing Him your sins!
For your souls' health, I'll absolution give;
So, though you die, blest martyrs shall you live,
Thrones you shall win in the great Paradis."
The Franks dismount, upon the ground are lit.
That Archbishop God's Benediction gives,
For their penance, good blows to strike he bids.

XC

The Franks arise, and stand upon their feet,
They're well absolved, and from their sins made clean,
And the Archbishop has signed them with God's seal;
And next they mount upon their chargers keen;
By rule of knights they have put on their gear,
For battle all apparelled as is meet.
The count Rollant calls Oliver, and speaks:
"Comrade and friend, now clearly have you seen
That Guenelun hath got us by deceit;
Gold hath he ta'en; much wealth is his to keep;
That Emperour vengeance for us must wreak.

King Marsilies hath bargained for us cheap;
At the sword's point he yet shall pay our meed." AOI.

XCI

To Spanish pass is Rollant now going
On Veillantif, his good steed, galloping;
He is well armed, pride is in his bearing,
He goes, so brave, his spear in hand holding,
He goes, its point against the sky turning;
A gonfalon all white thereon he's pinned,
Down to his hand flutters the golden fringe:
Noble his limbs, his face clear and smiling.
His companion goes after, following,
The men of France their warrant find in him.
Proudly he looks towards the Sarrazins,
And to the Franks sweetly, himself humbling;
And courteously has said to them this thing:
"My lords barons, go now your pace holding!
Pagans are come great martyrdom seeking;
Noble and fair reward this day shall bring,
Was never won by any Frankish King."
Upon these words the hosts are come touching. AOI.

XCII

Speaks Oliver: "No more now will I say.
Your olifant, to sound it do not deign,
Since from Carlun you'll never more have aid.
He has not heard; no fault of his, so brave.
Those with him there are never to be blamed.
So canter on, with what prowess you may!
Lords and barons, firmly your ground maintain!
Be minded well, I pray you in God's Name,
Stout blows to strike, to give as you shall take.
Forget the cry of Charles we never may."
Upon this word the Franks cry out amain.

Who then had heard them all "Monjoie!" acclaim,
Of vassalage might well recall the tale.
They canter forth, God! with what proud parade,
Pricking their spurs, the better speed to gain;
They go to strike,—what other thing could they?—
But Sarrazins are not at all afraid.
Pagans and Franks, you'ld see them now engaged.

XCIII

Marsile's nephew, his name is Aëlroth,
First of them all canters before the host,
Says of our Franks these ill words as he goes:
"Felons of France, so here on us you close!
Betrayed you has he that to guard you ought!
Mad is the King who left you in this post.
So shall the fame of France the Douce be lost,
And the right arm from Charlè's body torn."
When Rollant hears, what rage he has, by God!
His steed he spurs, gallops with great effort;
He goes, that count, to strike with all his force,
The shield he breaks, the hauberk's seam unsews,
Slices the heart, and shatters up the bones,
All of the spine he severs with that blow,
And with his spear the soul from body throws
So well he's pinned, he shakes in the air that corse,
On his spear's hilt he's flung it from the horse:
So in two halves Aëlroth's neck he broke,
Nor left him yet, they say, but rather spoke:
"Avaunt, culvert! A madman Charles is not,
No treachery was ever in his thought.
Proudly he did, who left us in this post;
The fame of France the Douce shall not be lost.
Strike on, the Franks! Ours are the foremost blows.
For we are right, but these gluttons are wrong." AOI.

XCIV

A duke there was, his name was Falfarun,
Brother was he to King Marsiliun,
He held their land, Dathan's and Abirun's;
Beneath the sky no more encrimed felun;
Between his eyes so broad was he in front
A great half-foot you'ld measure there in full.
His nephew dead he's seen with grief enough,
Comes through the press and wildly forth he runs,
Aloud he shouts their cry the pagans use;
And to the Franks is right contrarious:
"Honour of France the Douce shall fall to us!"
Hears Oliver, he's very furious,
His horse he pricks with both his golden spurs,
And goes to strike, ev'n as a baron doth;
The shield he breaks and through the hauberk cuts,
His ensign's fringe into the carcass thrusts,
On his spear's hilt he's flung it dead in dust.
Looks on the ground, sees glutton lying thus,
And says to him, with reason proud enough:
"From threatening, culvert, your mouth I've shut.
Strike on, the Franks! Right well we'll overcome."
"Monjoie," he shouts, 'twas the ensign of Carlun. AOI.

XCV

A king there was, his name was Corsablix,
Barbarian, and of a strange country,
He's called aloud to the other Sarrazins:
"Well may we join battle upon this field,
For of the Franks but very few are here;
And those are here, we should account them cheap,
From Charles not one has any warranty.
This is the day when they their death shall meet."
Has heard him well that Archbishop Turpin,

No man he'ld hate so much the sky beneath;
Spurs of fine gold he pricks into his steed,
To strike that king by virtue great goes he,
The hauberk all unfastens, breaks the shield,
Thrusts his great spear in through the carcass clean,
Pins it so well he shakes it in its seat,
Dead in the road he's flung it from his spear.
Looks on the ground, that glutton lying sees,
Nor leaves him yet, they say, but rather speaks:
"Culvert pagan, you lied now in your teeth,
Charlès my lord our warrant is indeed;
None of our Franks hath any mind to flee.
Your companions all on this spot we'll keep,
I tell you news; death shall ye suffer here.
Strike on, the Franks! Fail none of you at need!
Ours the first blow, to God the glory be!"
"Monjoie!" he cries, for all the camp to hear.

XCVI

And Gerins strikes Malprimis of Brigal
So his good shield is nothing worth at all,
Shatters the boss, was fashioned of crystal,
One half of it downward to earth flies off;
Right to the flesh has through his hauberk torn,
On his good spear he has the carcass caught.
And with one blow that pagan downward falls;
The soul of him Satan away hath borne. AOI.

XCVII

And his comrade Gerers strikes the admiral,
The shield he breaks, the hauberk unmetals,
And his good spear drives into his vitals,
So well he's pinned him, clean through the carcass,
Dead on the field he's flung him from his hand.
Says Oliver: "Now is our battle grand."

XCVIII

Sansun the Duke goes strike that almacour,
The shield he breaks, with golden flowers tooled,
That good hauberk for him is nothing proof,
He's sliced the heart, the lungs and liver through,
And flung him dead, as well or ill may prove.
Says the Archbishop: "A baron's stroke, in truth."

XCIX

And Anséis has let his charger run;
He goes to strike Turgis of Turtelus,
The shield he breaks, its golden boss above,
The hauberk too, its doubled mail undoes,
His good spear's point into the carcass runs,
So well he's thrust, clean through the whole steel comes,
And from the hilt he's thrown him dead in dust.
Then says Rollant: "Great prowess in that thrust."

C

And Engelers the Gascoin of Burdele
Spurs on his horse, lets fall the reins as well,
He goes to strike Escremiz of Valtrene,
The shield he breaks and shatters on his neck,
The hauberk too, he has its chinguard rent,
Between the arm-pits has pierced him through the breast,
On his spear's hilt from saddle throws him dead;
After he says: "So are you turned to hell." AOI.

CI

And Otès strikes a pagan Estorgant
Upon the shield, before its leathern band,
Slices it through, the white with the scarlat;
The hauberk too, has torn its folds apart,
And his good spear thrusts clean through the carcass,
And flings it dead, ev'n as the horse goes past;
He says: "You have no warrant afterward."

CII

And Berenger, he strikes Estramariz,
The shield he breaks, the hauberk tears and splits,
Thrusts his stout spear through's middle, and him flings
Down dead among a thousand Sarrazins.
Of their dozen peers ten have now been killed,
No more than two remain alive and quick,
Being Chernuble, and the count Margariz.

CIII

Margariz is a very gallant knight,
Both fair and strong, and swift he is and light;
He spurs his horse, goes Oliver to strike,
And breaks his shield, by th' golden buckle bright;
Along his ribs the pagan's spear doth glide;
God's his warrant, his body has respite,
The shaft breaks off, Oliver stays upright;
That other goes, naught stays him in his flight,
His trumpet sounds, rallies his tribe to fight.

CIV

Common the fight is now and marvellous.
The count Rollant no way himself secures,
Strikes with his spear, long as the shaft endures,
By fifteen blows it is clean broken through;
Then Durendal he bares, his sabre good
Spurs on his horse, is gone to strike Chernuble,
The helmet breaks, where bright carbuncles grew,
Slices the cap and shears the locks in two,
Slices also the eyes and the features,
The hauberk white, whose mail was close of woof,
Down to the groin cuts all his body through
To the saddle; with beaten gold 'twas tooled.
Upon the horse that sword a moment stood,
Then sliced its spine, no join there any knew,

Dead in the field among thick grass them threw.
After he said: "Culvert, false step you moved,
From Mahumet your help will not come soon.
No victory for gluttons such as you."

CV

The count Rollant, he canters through the field,
Holds Durendal, he well can thrust and wield,
Right great damage he's done the Sarrazines
You'd seen them, one on other, dead in heaps,
Through all that place their blood was flowing clear!
In blood his arms were and his hauberk steeped,
And bloodied o'er, shoulders and neck, his steed.
And Oliver goes on to strike with speed;
No blame that way deserve the dozen peers,
For all the Franks they strike and slay with heat,
Pagans are slain, some swoon there in their seats;
Says the Archbishop: "Good baronage indeed!"
"Monjoie" he cries, the call of Charles repeats. AOI.

CVI

And Oliver has cantered through the crush;
Broken his spear, the truncheon still he thrusts;
Going to strike a pagan Malsarun;
Flowers and gold, are on the shield, he cuts,
Out of the head both the two eyes have burst,
And all the brains are fallen in the dust;
He flings him dead, sev'n hundred else amongst.
Then has he slain Turgis and Esturgus;
Right to the hilt, his spear in flinders flew.
Then says Rollant: "Companion, what do you?
In such a fight, there's little strength in wood,
Iron and steel should here their valour prove.
Where is your sword, that Halteclere I knew?
Golden its hilt, whereon a crystal grew."

Says Oliver: "I had not, if I drew,
Time left to strike enough good blows and true." AOI.

CVII

Then Oliver has drawn his mighty sword
As his comrade had bidden and implored,
In knightly wise the blade to him has shewed;
Justin he strikes, that Iron Valley's lord,
All of his head has down the middle shorn,
The carcass sliced, the broidered sark has torn,
The good saddle that was with gold adorned,
And through the spine has sliced that pagan's horse;
Dead in the field before his feet they fall.
Says Rollant: "Now my brother I you call;
He'll love us for such blows, our Emperor."
On every side "Monjoie" you'ld hear them roar. AOI.

CVIII

That count Gerins sate on his horse Sorel,
On Passe-Cerf was Gerers there, his friend;
They've loosed their reins, together spurred and sped,
And go to strike a pagan Timozel;
One on the shield, on hauberk the other fell;
And their two spears went through the carcass well,
A fallow field amidst they've thrown him dead.
I do not know, I never heard it said
Which of the two was nimbler as they went.
Esperveris was there, son of Borel,
And him there slew Engelers of Burdel.
And the Archbishop, he slew them Siglorel,
The enchanter, who before had been in hell,
Where Jupiter bore him by a magic spell.
Then Turpin says: "To us he's forfeited."
Answers Rollant: "The culvert is bested.
Such blows, brother Olivier, I like well."

CIX

The battle grows more hard and harder yet,
Franks and pagans, with marvellous onset,
Each other strike and each himself defends.
So many shafts bloodstained and shatterèd,
So many flags and ensigns tatterèd;
So many Franks lose their young lustihead,
Who'll see no more their mothers nor their friends,
Nor hosts of France, that in the pass attend.
Charlès the Great weeps therefor with regret.
What profits that? No succour shall they get.
Evil service, that day, Guenes rendered them,
To Sarraguce going, his own to sell.
After he lost his members and his head,
In court, at Aix, to gallows-tree condemned;
And thirty more with him, of his kindred,
Were hanged, a thing they never did expect. AOI.

CX

Now marvellous and weighty the combat,
Right well they strike, Olivier and Rollant,
A thousand blows come from the Archbishop's hand,
The dozen peers are nothing short of that,
With one accord join battle all the Franks.
Pagans are slain by hundred, by thousand,
Who flies not then, from death has no warrant,
Will he or nill, foregoes the allotted span.
The Franks have lost the foremost of their band,
They'll see no more their fathers nor their clans,
Nor Charlemagne, where in the pass he stands.
Torment arose, right marvellous, in France,
Tempest there was, of wind and thunder black,
With rain and hail, so much could not be spanned;
Fell thunderbolts often on every hand,

And verily the earth quaked in answer back
From Saint Michael of Peril unto Sanz,
From Besençun to the harbour of Guitsand;
No house stood there but straight its walls must crack:
In full mid-day the darkness was so grand,
Save the sky split, no light was in the land.
Beheld these things with terror every man,
And many said: "We in the Judgement stand;
The end of time is presently at hand."
They spake no truth; they did not understand;
'Twas the great day of mourning for Rollant.

CXI

The Franks strike on; their hearts are good and stout.
Pagans are slain, a thousandfold, in crowds,
Left of five score are not two thousands now.
Says the Archbishop: "Our men are very proud,
No man on earth has more nor better found.
In Chronicles of Franks is written down,
What vassalage he had, our Emperour."
Then through the field they go, their friends seek out,
And their eyes weep with grief and pain profound
For kinsmen dear, by hearty friendship bound.
King Marsilies and his great host draw round. AOI.

CXII

King Marsilies along a valley led
The mighty host that he had gatherèd.
Twenty columns that king had numberèd.
With gleaming gold their helms were jewellèd.
Shone too their shields and sarks embroiderèd.
Sounded the charge seven thousand trumpets,
Great was the noise through all that country went.
Then said Rollant: "Olivier, brother, friend,
That felon Guenes hath sworn to achieve our death;

For his treason no longer is secret.
Right great vengeance our Emperour will get.
Battle we'll have, both long and keenly set,
Never has man beheld such armies met.
With Durendal my sword I'll strike again,
And, comrade, you shall strike with Halteclere.
These swords in lands so many have we held,
Battles with them so many brought to end,
No evil song shall e'er be sung or said." AOI.

CXIII

When the Franks see so many there, pagans,
On every side covering all the land,
Often they call Olivier and Rollant,
The dozen peers, to be their safe warrant.
And the Archbishop speaks to them, as he can:
"My lords barons, go thinking nothing bad!
For God I pray you fly not hence but stand,
Lest evil songs of our valour men chant!
Far better 't were to perish in the van.
Certain it is, our end is near at hand,
Beyond this day shall no more live one man;
But of one thing I give you good warrant:
Blest Paradise to you now open stands,
By the Innocents your thrones you there shall have."
Upon these words grow bold again the Franks;
There is not one but he "Monjoie" demands. AOI.

CXIV

A Sarrazin was there, of Sarraguce,
Of that city one half was his by use,
'Twas Climborins, a man was nothing proof;
By Guenelun the count an oath he took,
And kissed his mouth in amity and truth,
Gave him his sword and his carbuncle too.

Terra Major, he said, to shame he'ld put,
From the Emperour his crown he would remove.
He sate his horse, which he called Barbamusche,
Never so swift sparrow nor swallow flew,
He spurred him well, and down the reins he threw,
Going to strike Engelier of Gascune;
Nor shield nor sark him any warrant proved,
The pagan spear's point did his body wound,
He pinned him well, and all the steel sent through,
From the hilt flung him dead beneath his foot.
After he said: "Good are they to confuse.
Pagans, strike on, and so this press set loose!"
"God!" say the Franks, "Grief, such a man to lose!"
AOI.

CXV

The count Rollant called upon Oliver:
"Sir companion, dead now is Engeler;
Than whom we'd no more valiant chevalier."
Answered that count: "God, let me him avenge!"
Spurs of fine gold into his horse drove then,
Held Halteclere, with blood its steel was red,
By virtue great to strike that pagan went,
Brandished his blade, the Sarrazin upset;
The Adversaries of God his soul bare thence.
Next he has slain the duke Alphaïen,
And sliced away Escababi his head,
And has unhorsed some seven Arabs else;
No good for those to go to war again.
Then said Rollant: "My comrade shews anger,
So in my sight he makes me prize him well;
More dear by Charles for such blows are we held."
Aloud he's cried: "Strike on, the chevaliers!"
AOI.

CXVI

From the other part a pagan Valdabron:
Warden he'd been to king Marsilion,
And lord, by sea, of four hundred dromonds;
No sailor was but called his name upon;
Jerusalem he'd taken by treason,
Violated the Temple of Salomon,
The Patriarch had slain before the fonts.
He'd pledged his oath by county Guenelon,
Gave him his sword, a thousand coins thereon.
He sate his horse, which he called Gramimond,
Never so swift flew in the air falcon;
He's pricked him well, with sharp spurs he had on,
Going to strike e'en that rich Duke, Sanson;
His shield has split, his hauberk has undone,
The ensign's folds have through his body gone,
Dead from the hilt out of his seat he's dropt:
"Pagans, strike on, for well we'll overcome!"
"God!" say the Franks, "Grief for a brave baron!" AOI.

CXVII

The count Rollant, when Sansun dead he saw,
You may believe, great grief he had therefor.
His horse he spurs, gallops with great effort,
Wields Durendal, was worth fine gold and more,
Goes as he may to strike that baron bold
Above the helm, that was embossed with gold,
Slices the head, the sark, and all the corse,
The good saddle, that was embossed with gold,
And cuts deep through the backbone of his horse;
He's slain them both, blame him for that or laud.
The pagans say: " 'Twas hard on us, that blow."
Answers Rollant: "Nay, love you I can not,
For on your side is arrogance and wrong." AOI.

CXVIII

Out of Affrike an Affrican was come,
'Twas Malquiant, the son of king Malcud;
With beaten gold was all his armour done,
Fore all men's else it shone beneath the sun.
He sate his horse, which he called Salt-Perdut,
Never so swift was any beast could run.
And Anséis upon the shield he struck,
The scarlat with the blue he sliced it up,
Of his hauberk he's torn the folds and cut,
The steel and stock has through his body thrust.
Dead is that count, he's no more time to run.
Then say the Franks: "Baron, an evil luck!"

CXIX

Swift through the field Turpin the Archbishop passed;
Such shaven-crown has never else sung Mass
Who with his limbs such prowess might compass;
To th' pagan said: "God send thee all that's bad!
One thou hast slain for whom my heart is sad."
So his good horse forth at his bidding ran,
He's struck him then on his shield Toledan,
Until he flings him dead on the green grass.

CXX

From the other part was a pagan Grandones,
Son of Capuel, the king of Capadoce.
He sate his horse, the which he called Marmore,
Never so swift was any bird in course;
He's loosed the reins, and spurring on that horse
He's gone to strike Gerin with all his force;
The scarlat shield from's neck he's broken off,
And all his sark thereafter has he torn,
The ensign blue clean through his body's gone,
Until he flings him dead, on a high rock;

His companion Gerer he's slain also,
And Berenger, and Guiun of Santone;
Next a rich duke he's gone to strike, Austore,
That held Valence and the Honour of the Rhone;
He's flung him dead; great joy the pagans shew.
Then say the Franks: "Of ours how many fall."

CXXI

The count Rollant, his sword with blood is stained,
Well has he heard what way the Franks complained;
Such grief he has, his heart would split in twain:
To the pagan says: "God send thee every shame!
One hast thou slain that dearly thou'lt repay."
He spurs his horse, that on with speed doth strain;
Which should forfeit, they both together came.

CXXII

Grandonie was both proof and valiant,
And virtuous, a vassal combatant.
Upon the way there, he has met Rollant;
He'd never seen, yet knew him at a glance,
By the proud face and those fine limbs he had,
By his regard, and by his countenance;
He could not help but he grew faint thereat,
He would escape, nothing avail he can.
Struck him the count, with so great virtue, that
To the nose-plate he's all the helmet cracked,
Sliced through the nose and mouth and teeth he has,
Hauberk close-mailed, and all the whole carcass,
Saddle of gold, with plates of silver flanked,
And of his horse has deeply scarred the back;
He's slain them both, they'll make no more attack:
The Spanish men in sorrow cry, "Alack!"
Then say the Franks: "He strikes well, our warrant."

CXXIII

Marvellous is the battle in its speed,
The Franks there strike with vigour and with heat,
Cutting through wrists and ribs and chines indeed,
Through garments to the lively flesh beneath;
On the green grass the clear blood runs in streams.
The pagans say: "No more we'll suffer, we.
Terra Major, Mahummet's curse on thee!
Beyond all men thy people are hardy!"
There was not one but cried then: "Marsilie,
Canter, o king, thy succour now we need!"

CXXIV

Marvellous is the battle now and grand,
The Franks there strike, their good brown spears in hand.
Then had you seen such sorrowing of clans,
So many a slain, shattered and bleeding man!
Biting the earth, or piled there on their backs!
The Sarrazins cannot such loss withstand.
Will they or nill, from off the field draw back;
By lively force chase them away the Franks. AOI.

CXXV

Their martyrdom, his men's, Marsile has seen,
So he bids sound his horns and his buccines;
Then canters forth with all his great army.
Canters before a Sarrazin, Abisme,
More felon none was in that company;
Cankered with guile and every felony,
He fears not God, the Son of Saint Mary;
Black is that man as molten pitch that seethes;
Better he loves murder and treachery
Than to have all the gold of Galicie;
Never has man beheld him sport for glee;
Yet vassalage he's shown, and great folly,

So is he dear to th' felon king Marsile;
Dragon he bears, to which his tribe rally.
That Archbishop could never love him, he;
Seeing him there, to strike he's very keen,
Within himself he says all quietly:
"This Sarrazin great heretick meseems,
Rather I'ld die, than not slay him clean,
Ne'er did I love coward nor cowardice."   AOI.

CXXVI

That Archbishop begins the fight again,
Sitting the horse which he took from Grossaille,
That was a king he had in Denmark slain.
That charger is swift and of noble race;
Fine are his hooves, his legs are smooth and straight,
Short are his thighs, broad crupper he displays,
Long are his ribs, aloft his spine is raised,
White is his tail and yellow is his mane,
Little his ears, and tawny all his face;
No beast is there, can match him in a race.
That Archbishop spurs on by vassalage,
He will not pause ere Abisme he assail;
So strikes that shield, is wonderfully arrayed,
Whereon are stones, amethyst and topaze,
Esterminals and carbuncles that blaze;
A devil's gift it was, in Val Metase,
Who handed it to the Admiral Galafes;
So Turpin strikes, spares him not anyway;
After that blow, he's worth no penny wage;
The carcass he's sliced, rib from rib away,
So flings him down dead in an empty place.
Then say the Franks: "He has great vassalage,
With the Archbishop, surely the Cross is safe."

CXXVII

The count Rollant calls upon Oliver:
"Sir companion, witness you'll freely bear,
The Archbishop is a right good chevalier,
None better is neath Heaven anywhere;
Well can he strike with lance and well with spear."
Answers that count: "Support to him we'll bear!"
Upon that word the Franks again make yare;
Hard are the blows, slaughter and suffering there,
For Christians too, most bitter grief and care.
Who could had seen Rollant and Oliver
With their good swords to strike and to slaughter!
And the Archbishop lays on there with his spear.
Those that are dead, men well may hold them dear.
In charters and in briefs is written clear,
Four thousand fell, and more, the tales declare.
Gainst four assaults easily did they fare,
But then the fifth brought heavy griefs to bear.
They all are slain, those Frankish chevaliers;
Only three-score, whom God was pleased to spare,
Before these die, they'll sell them very dear. AOI.

CXXVIII

The count Rollant great loss of his men sees,
His companion Olivier calls, and speaks:
"Sir and comrade, in God's Name, That you keeps,
Such good vassals you see lie here in heaps;
For France the Douce, fair country, may we weep,
Of such barons long desolate she'll be.
Ah! King and friend, wherefore are you not here?
How, Oliver, brother, can we achieve?
And by what means our news to him repeat?"
Says Oliver: "I know not how to seek;
Rather I'ld die than shame come of this feat." AOI.

CXXIX

Then says Rollant: "I'll wind this olifant,
If Charlès hear, where in the pass he stands,
I pledge you now they will return, the Franks."
Says Oliver: "Great shame would come of that;
And a reproach on every one, your clan,
That shall endure while each lives in the land,
When I implored, you would not do this act;
Doing it now, no praise from me you'll have:
So wind your horn, but not by courage rash,
Seeing that both your arms with blood are splashed."
Answers that count: "Fine blows I've struck them back."
AOI.

CXXX

Then says Rollant: "Strong it is now, our battle;
I'll wind my horn, so the King hears it, Charlès."
Says Oliver: "That act were not a vassal's.
When I implored you, comrade, you were wrathful.
Were the King here, we had not borne such damage.
Nor should we blame those with him there, his army."
Says Oliver: "Now by my beard, hereafter
If I may see my gentle sister Alde,
She in her arms, I swear, shall never clasp you." AOI.

CXXXI

Then says Rollant: "Wherefore so wroth with me?"
He answers him: "Comrade, it was your deed:
Vassalage comes by sense, and not folly;
Prudence more worth is than stupidity.
Here are Franks dead, all for your trickery;
No more service to Carlun may we yield.
My lord were here now, had you trusted me,
And fought and won this battle then had we,
Taken or slain were the king Marsilie.

In your prowess, Rollant, no good we've seen!
Charlès the great in vain your aid will seek—
None such as he till God His Judgement speak;—
Here must you die, and France in shame be steeped;
Here perishes our loyal company,
Before this night great severance and grief." AOI.

CXXXII

That Archbishop has heard them, how they spoke,
His horse he pricks with his fine spurs of gold,
Coming to them he takes up his reproach:
"Sir Oliver, and you, Sir Rollant, both,
For God I pray, do not each other scold!
No help it were to us, the horn to blow,
But, none the less, it may be better so;
The King will come, with vengeance that he owes;
These Spanish men never away shall go.
Our Franks here, each descending from his horse,
Will find us dead, and limb from body torn;
They'll take us hence, on biers and litters borne;
With pity and with grief for us they'll mourn;
They'll bury each in some old minster-close;
No wolf nor swine nor dog shall gnaw our bones."
Answers Rollant: "Sir, very well you spoke." AOI.

CXXXIII

Rollant hath set the olifant to his mouth,
He grasps it well, and with great virtue sounds.
High are those peaks, afar it rings and loud,
Thirty great leagues they hear its echoes mount.
So Charlès heard, and all his comrades round;
Then said that King: "Battle they do, our counts."
And Guenelun answered, contrarious:
"That were a lie, in any other mouth." AOI.

CXXXIV

The Count Rollant, with sorrow and with pangs,
And with great pain sounded his olifant:
Out of his mouth the clear blood leaped and ran,
About his brain the very temples cracked.
Loud is its voice, that horn he holds in hand;
Charlès hath heard, where in the pass he stands,
And Neimès hears, and listen all the Franks.
Then says the King: "I hear his horn, Rollant's;
He'ld never sound, but he were in combat."
Answers him Guenes: "It is no battle, that.
Now are you old, blossoming white and blanched,
Yet by such words you still appear infant.
You know full well the great pride of Rollant;
Marvel it is, God stays so tolerant.
Noples he took, not waiting your command;
Thence issued forth the Sarrazins, a band
With vassalage had fought against Rollant;
1777A He slew them first, with Durendal his brand,
Then washed their blood with water from the land;
So what he'd done might not be seen of man.
He for a hare goes all day, horn in hand;
Before his peers in foolish jest he brags.
No race neath heav'n in field him dare attack.
So canter on! Nay, wherefore hold we back?
Terra Major is far away, our land." AOI.

CXXXV

The count Rollant, though blood his mouth doth stain,
And burst are both the temples of his brain,
His olifant he sounds with grief and pain;
Charlès hath heard, listen the Franks again.
"That horn," the King says, "hath a mighty strain!"
Answers Duke Neimes: "A baron blows with pain!

Battle is there, indeed I see it plain,
He is betrayed, by one that still doth feign.
Equip you, sir, cry out your old refrain,
That noble band, go succour them amain!
Enough you've heard how Rollant doth complain."

CXXXVI

That Emperour hath bid them sound their horns.
The Franks dismount, and dress themselves for war,
Put hauberks on, helmets and golden swords;
Fine shields they have, and spears of length and force
Scarlat and blue and white their ensigns float.
His charger mounts each baron of the host;
They spur with haste as through the pass they go.
Nor was there one but thus to 's neighbour spoke:
"Now, ere he die, may we see Rollant, so
Ranged by his side we'll give some goodly blows."
But what avail? They've stayed too long below.

CXXXVII

That even-tide is light as was the day;
Their armour shines beneath the sun's clear ray,
Hauberks and helms throw off a dazzling flame,
And blazoned shields, flowered in bright array,
Also their spears, with golden ensigns gay.
That Emperour, he canters on with rage,
And all the Franks with wonder and dismay;
There is not one can bitter tears restrain,
And for Rollant they're very sore afraid.
The King has bid them seize that county Guene,
And charged with him the scullions of his train;
The master-cook he's called, Besgun by name:
"Guard me him well, his felony is plain,
Who in my house vile treachery has made."
He holds him, and a hundred others takes

From the kitchen, both good and evil knaves;
Then Guenè's beard and both his cheeks they shaved,
And four blows each with their closed fists they gave,
They trounced him well with cudgels and with staves,
And on his neck they clasped an iron chain;
So like a bear enchained they held him safe,
On a pack-mule they set him in his shame:
Kept him till Charles should call for him again.
AOI.

CXXXVIII

High were the peaks and shadowy and grand,
The valleys deep, the rivers swiftly ran.
Trumpets they blew in rear and in the van,
Till all again answered that olifant.
That Emperour canters with fury mad,
And all the Franks dismay and wonder have;
There is not one but weeps and waxes sad
And all pray God that He will guard Rollant
Till in the field together they may stand;
There by his side they'll strike as well they can.
But what avail? No good there is in that;
They're not in time; too long have they held back.
AOI.

CXXXIX

In his great rage on canters Charlemagne;
Over his sark his beard is flowing plain.
Barons of France, in haste they spur and strain;
There is not one that can his wrath contain
That they are not with Rollant the Captain,
Whereas he fights the Sarrazins of Spain.
If he be struck, will not one soul remain.
God! Sixty men are all now in his train!
Never a king had better Capitains. AOI.

CXL

Rollant regards the barren mountain-sides;
Dead men of France, he sees so many lie,
And weeps for them as fits a gentle knight:
"Lords and barons, may God to you be kind!
And all your souls redeem for Paradise!
And let you there mid holy flowers lie!
Better vassals than you saw never I.
Ever you've served me, and so long a time,
By you Carlon hath conquered kingdoms wide;
That Emperour reared you for evil plight!
Douce land of France, o very precious clime,
Laid desolate by such a sour exile!
Barons of France, for me I've seen you die,
And no support, no warrant could I find;
God be your aid, Who never yet hath lied!
I must not fail now, brother, by your side;
Save I be slain, for sorrow shall I die.
Sir companion, let us again go strike!"

CXLI

The count Rollant, back to the field then hieing
Holds Durendal, and like a vassal striking,
Faldrun of Pui has through the middle slicèd,
With twenty-four of all they rated highest;
Was never man, for vengeance shewed such liking.
Even as a stag before the hounds goes flying,
Before Rollant the pagans scatter, frightened.
Says the Archbishop: "You deal now very wisely!
Such valour should he shew that is bred knightly,
And beareth arms, and a good charger rideth;
In battle should be strong and proud and sprightly;
Or otherwise he is not worth a shilling,
Should be a monk in one of those old minsters,

Where, day by day, he'ld pray for us poor sinners."
Answers Rollant: "Strike on; no quarter give them!"
Upon these words Franks are again beginning;
Very great loss they suffer then, the Christians.

CXLII

The man who knows, for him there's no prison,
In such a fight with keen defence lays on;
Wherefore the Franks are fiercer than lions.
Marsile you'd seen go as a brave baron,
Sitting his horse, the which he calls Gaignon;
He spurs it well, going to strike Bevon,
That was the lord of Beaune and of Dijon,
His shield he breaks, his hauberk has undone,
So flings him dead, without condition;
Next he hath slain Yvoerie and Ivon,
Also with them Gerard of Russillon.
The count Rollant, being not far him from,
To th' pagan says: "Confound thee our Lord God!
So wrongfully you've slain my companions,
A blow you'll take, ere we apart be gone,
And of my sword the name I'll bid you con."
He goes to strike him, as a brave baron,
And his right hand the count clean slices off;
Then takes the head of Jursaleu the blond;
That was the son of King Marsilion.
Pagans cry out: "Assist us now, Mahom!
God of our race, avenge us on Carlon!
Into this land he's sent us such felons
That will not leave the fight before they drop."
Says each to each: "Nay let us fly!" Upon
That word, they're fled, an hundred thousand gone;
Call them who may, they'll never more come on.
AOI.

CXLIII

But what avail? Though fled be Marsilies,
He's left behind his uncle, the alcaliph
Who holds Alferne, Kartagene, Garmalie,
And Ethiope, a cursèd land indeed;
The blackamoors from there are in his keep,
Broad in the nose they are and flat in the ear,
Fifty thousand and more in company.
These canter forth with arrogance and heat,
Then they cry out the pagans' rallying cheer;
And Rollant says: "Martyrdom we'll receive;
Not long to live, I know it well, have we;
Felon he's named that sells his body cheap!
Strike on, my lords, with burnished swords and keen;
Contest each inch your life and death between,
That ne'er by us Douce France in shame be steeped.
When Charles my lord shall come into this field,
Such discipline of Sarrazins he'll see,
For one of ours he'll find them dead fifteen;
He will not fail, but bless us all in peace." AOI.

CXLIV

When Rollant sees those misbegotten men,
Who are more black than ink is on the pen
With no part white, only their teeth except,
Then says that count: "I know now very well
That here to die we're bound, as I can tell.
Strike on, the Franks! For so I recommend."
Says Oliver: "Who holds back, is condemned!"
Upon those words, the Franks do strike again.

CXLV

Franks are but few; which, when the pagans know,
Among themselves comfort and pride they shew;
Says each to each: "Wrong was that Emperor."

Their alcaliph upon a sorrel rode,
And pricked it well with both his spurs of gold;
Struck Oliver, behind, on the back-bone,
His hauberk white into his body broke,
Clean through his breast the thrusting spear he drove;
After he said: "You've borne a mighty blow.
Charlès the great should not have left you so;
He's done us wrong, small thanks to him we owe;
I've well avenged all ours on you alone."

CXLVI

Oliver feels that he to die is bound,
Holds Halteclere, whose steel is rough and brown,
Strikes the alcaliph on his helm's golden mount;
Flowers and stones fall clattering to the ground,
Slices his head, to th' small teeth in his mouth;
So brandishes his blade and flings him down;
After he says: "Pagan, accurst be thou!
Thou'lt never say that Charles forsakes me now;
Nor to thy wife, nor any dame thou'st found,
Thou'lt never boast, in lands where thou wast crowned,
One pennyworth from me thou'st taken out,
Nor damage wrought on me nor any around."
After, for aid, "Rollant!" he cries aloud. AOI.

CXLVII

Oliver feels that death is drawing nigh;
To avenge himself he hath no longer time;
Through the great press most gallantly he strikes,
He breaks their spears, their buckled shields doth slice,
Their feet, their fists, their shoulders and their sides,
Dismembers them: whoso had seen that sight,
Dead in the field one on another piled,
Remember well a vassal brave he might.
Charlè's ensign he'll not forget it quite;

Aloud and clear "Monjoie" again he cries.
To call Rollant, his friend and peer, he tries:
"My companion, come hither to my side.
With bitter grief we must us now divide." AOI.

CXLVIII

Then Rollant looked upon Olivier's face;
Which was all wan and colourless and pale,
While the clear blood, out of his body sprayed,
Upon the ground gushed forth and ran away.
"God!" said that count, "What shall I do or say?
My companion, gallant for such ill fate!
Ne'er shall man be, against thee could prevail.
Ah! France the Douce, henceforth art thou made waste
Of vassals brave, confounded and disgraced!
Our Emperour shall suffer damage great."
And with these words upon his horse he faints. AOI.

CXLIX

You'd seen Rollant aswoon there in his seat,
And Oliver, who unto death doth bleed,
So much he's bled, his eyes are dim and weak;
Nor clear enough his vision, far or near,
To recognise whatever man he sees;
His companion, when each the other meets,
Above the helm jewelled with gold he beats,
Slicing it down from there to the nose-piece,
But not his head; he's touched not brow nor cheek.
At such a blow Rollant regards him keen,
And asks of him, in gentle tones and sweet:
"To do this thing, my comrade, did you mean?
This is Rollant, who ever held you dear;
And no mistrust was ever us between."
Says Oliver: "Now can I hear you speak;
I see you not: may the Lord God you keep!

I struck you now: and for your pardon plead."
Answers Rollant: "I am not hurt, indeed;
I pardon you, before God's Throne and here."
Upon these words, each to the other leans;
And in such love you had their parting seen.

CL

Oliver feels death's anguish on him now;
And in his head his two eyes swimming round;
Nothing he sees; he hears not any sound;
Dismounting then, he kneels upon the ground,
Proclaims his sins both firmly and aloud,
Clasps his two hands, heavenwards holds them out,
Prays God himself in Paradise to allow;
Blessings on Charles, and on Douce France he vows,
And his comrade, Rollant, to whom he's bound.
Then his heart fails; his helmet nods and bows;
Upon the earth he lays his whole length out:
And he is dead, may stay no more, that count.
Rollant the brave mourns him with grief profound;
Nowhere on earth so sad a man you'd found.

CLI

So Rollant's friend is dead; whom when he sees
Face to the ground, and biting it with 's teeth,
Begins to mourn in language very sweet:
"Unlucky, friend, your courage was indeed!
Together we have spent such days and years;
No harmful thing twixt thee and me has been.
Now thou art dead, and all my life a grief."
And with these words again he swoons, that chief,
Upon his horse, which he calls Veillantif;
Stirrups of gold support him underneath;
He cannot fall, whichever way he lean.

CLII

Soon as Rollant his senses won and knew,
Recovering and turning from that swoon.
Bitter great loss appeared there in his view:
Dead are the Franks; he'd all of them to lose,
Save the Archbishop, and save Gualter del Hum;
He is come down out of the mountains, who
Gainst Spanish men made there a great ado;
Dead are his men, for those the pagans slew;
Will he or nill, along the vales he flew,
And called Rollant, to bring him succour soon:
"Ah! Gentle count, brave soldier, where are you?
For by thy side no fear I ever knew.
Gualter it is, who conquered Maëlgut,
And nephew was to hoary old Droün;
My vassalage thou ever thoughtest good.
Broken my spear, and split my shield in two;
Gone is the mail that on my hauberk grew;
This body of mine eight lances have gone through;
I'm dying. Yet full price for life I took."
Rollant has heard these words and understood,
Has spurred his horse, and on towards him drew. AOI.

CLIII

Grief gives Rollant intollerance and pride;
Through the great press he goes again to strike;
To slay a score of Spaniards he contrives,
Gualter has six, the Archbishop other five.
The pagans say: "Men, these, of felon kind!
Lordings, take care they go not hence alive!
Felon he's named that does not break their line,
Recreant, who lets them any safety find!"
And so once more begin the hue and cry,
From every part they come to break the line. AOI.

CLIV

Count Rollant is a noble and brave soldier,
Gualter del Hum's a right good chevalier,
That Archbishop hath shewn good prowess there;
None of them falls behind the other pair;
Through the great press, pagans they strike again.
Come on afoot a thousand Sarrazens,
And on horseback some forty thousand men.
But well I know, to approach they never dare;
Lances and spears they poise to hurl at them,
Arrows, barbs, darts and javelins in the air.
With their first flight they've slain our Gualtïer;
Turpin of Reims has all his shield broken,
And cracked his helm; he's wounded in the head,
From his hauberk the woven mail they tear,
In his body four spear-wounds doth he bear;
Beneath him too his charger's fallen dead.
Great grief it was, when that Archbishop fell. AOI.

CLV

Turpin of Reims hath felt himself undone,
Since that four spears have through his body come;
Nimble and bold upon his feet he jumps;
Looks for Rollant, and then towards him runs,
Saying this word: "I am not overcome.
While life remains, no good vassal gives up."
He's drawn Almace, whose steel was brown and rough,
Through the great press a thousand blows he's struck:
As Charlès said, quarter he gave to none;
He found him there, four hundred else among,
Wounded the most, speared through the middle some,
Also there were from whom the heads he'd cut:
So tells the tale, he that was there says thus,
The brave Saint Giles, whom God made marvellous,

Who charters wrote for th' Minster at Loüm;
Nothing he's heard that does not know this much.

CLVI

The count Rollant has nobly fought and well,
But he is hot, and all his body sweats;
Great pain he has, and trouble in his head,
His temples burst when he the horn sounded;
But he would know if Charles will come to them,
Takes the olifant, and feebly sounds again.
That Emperour stood still and listened then:
"My lords," said he, "Right evilly we fare!
This day Rollant, my nephew shall be dead:
I hear his horn, with scarcely any breath.
Nimbly canter, whoever would be there!
Your trumpets sound, as many as ye bear!"
Sixty thousand so loud together blare,
The mountains ring, the valleys answer them.
The pagans hear, they think it not a jest;
Says each to each: "Carlum doth us bestead." AOI.

CLVII

The pagans say: "That Emperour's at hand,
We hear their sound, the trumpets of the Franks;
If Charlès come, great loss we then shall stand,
And wars renewed, unless we slay Rollant;
All Spain we'll lose, our own clear father-land."
Four hundred men of them in helmets stand;
The best of them that might be in their ranks
Make on Rollant a grim and fierce attack;
Gainst these the count had well enough in hand. AOI.

CLVIII

The count Rollant, when their approach he sees
Is grown so bold and manifest and fierce
So long as he's alive he will not yield.

He sits his horse, which men call Veillantif,
Pricking him well with golden spurs beneath,
Through the great press he goes, their line to meet,
And by his side is the Archbishop Turpin.
"Now, friend, begone!" say pagans, each to each;
"These Frankish men, their horns we plainly hear;
Charle is at hand, that King in Majesty."

CLIX

The count Rollant has never loved cowards,
Nor arrogant, nor men of evil heart,
Nor chevalier that was not good vassal.
That Archbishop, Turpin, he calls apart:
"Sir, you're afoot, and I my charger have;
For love of you, here will I take my stand,
Together we'll endure things good and bad;
I'll leave you not, for no incarnate man:
We'll give again these pagans their attack;
The better blows are those from Durendal."
Says the Archbishop: "Shame on him that holds back!
Charles is at hand, full vengeance he'll exact."

CLX

The pagans say: "Unlucky were we born!
An evil day for us did this day dawn!
For we have lost our peers and all our lords.
Charles his great host once more upon us draws,
Of Frankish men we plainly hear the horns,
"Monjoie" they cry, and great is their uproar.
The count Rollant is of such pride and force
He'll never yield to man of woman born;
Let's aim at him, then leave him on the spot!"
And aim they did: with arrows long and short,
Lances and spears and feathered javelots;
Count Rollant's shield they've broken through and bored

The woven mail have from his hauberk torn,
But not himself, they've never touched his corse;
Veillantif is in thirty places gored,
Beneath the count he's fallen dead, that horse.
Pagans are fled, and leave him on the spot;
The count Rollant stands on his feet once more. AOI.

CLXI

Pagans are fled, enangered and enraged,
Home into Spain with speed they make their way;
The count Rollant, he has not given chase,
For Veillantif, his charger, they have slain;
Will he or nill, on foot he must remain.
To the Archbishop, Turpin, he goes with aid;
He's from his head the golden helm unlaced,
Taken from him his white hauberk away,
And cut the gown in strips, was round his waist;
On his great wounds the pieces of it placed,
Then to his heart has caught him and embraced;
On the green grass he has him softly laid,
Most sweetly then to him has Rollant prayed:
"Ah! Gentle sir, give me your leave, I say;
Our companions, whom we so dear appraised,
Are now all dead; we cannot let them stay;
I will go seek and bring them to this place,
Arrange them here in ranks, before your face."
Said the Archbishop: "Go, and return again.
This field is yours and mine now; God be praised!"

CLXII

So Rollant turns; through the field, all alone,
Searching the vales and mountains, he is gone;
He finds Gerin, Gerers his companion,
Also he finds Berenger and Otton,
There too he finds Anséis and Sanson,

And finds Gerard the old, of Rossillon;
By one and one he's taken those barons,
To the Archbishop with each of them he comes,
Before his knees arranges every one.
That Archbishop, he cannot help but sob,
He lifts his hand, gives benediction;
After he's said: "Unlucky, Lords, your lot!
But all your souls He'll lay, our Glorious God,
In Paradise, His holy flowers upon!
For my own death such anguish now I've got;
I shall not see him, our rich Emperour."

CLXIII

So Rollant turns, goes through the field in quest;
His companion Olivier finds at length;
He has embraced him close against his breast,
To the Archbishop returns as he can best;
Upon a shield he's laid him, by the rest;
And the Archbishop has them absolved and blest:
Whereon his grief and pity grow afresh.
Then says Rollant: "Fair comrade Olivier,
You were the son of the good count Reinier,
Who held the march by th' Vale of Runïer;
To shatter spears, through buckled shields to bear,
And from hauberks the mail to break and tear,
Proof men to lead, and prudent counsel share,
Gluttons in field to frighten and conquer,
No land has known a better chevalier."

CLXIV

The count Rollant, when dead he saw his peers,
And Oliver, he held so very dear,
Grew tender, and began to shed a tear;
Out of his face the colour disappeared;
No longer could he stand, for so much grief,

Will he or nill, he swooned upon the field.
Said the Archbishop: "Unlucky lord, indeed!"

CLXV

When the Archbishop beheld him swoon, Rollant,
Never before such bitter grief he'd had;
Stretching his hand, he took that olifant.
Through Rencesvals a little river ran;
He would go there, fetch water for Rollant.
Went step by step, to stumble soon began,
So feeble he is, no further fare he can,
For too much blood he's lost, and no strength has;
Ere he has crossed an acre of the land,
His heart grows faint, he falls down forwards and
Death comes to him with very cruel pangs.

CLXVI

The count Rollant wakes from his swoon once more,
Climbs to his feet; his pains are very sore;
Looks down the vale, looks to the hills above;
On the green grass, beyond his companions,
He sees him lie, that noble old baron;
'Tis the Archbishop, whom in His name wrought God.
There he proclaims his sins, and looks above;
Joins his two hands, to Heaven holds them forth,
And Paradise prays God to him to accord.
Dead is Turpin, the warrior of Charlon.
In battles great and very rare sermons
Against pagans ever a champion.
God grant him now His Benediction! AOI.

CLXVII

The count Rollant sees the Archbishop lie dead,
Sees the bowels out of his body shed,
And sees the brains that surge from his forehead;
Between his two arm-pits, upon his breast,

Crossways he folds those hands so white and fair.
Then mourns aloud, as was the custom there:
"Thee, gentle sir, chevalier nobly bred,
To the Glorious Celestial I commend;
Ne'er shall man be, that will Him serve so well;
Since the Apostles was never such prophet,
To hold the laws and draw the hearts of men.
Now may your soul no pain nor sorrow ken,
Finding the gates of Paradise open!"

CLXVIII

Then Rollant feels that death to him draws near,
For all his brain is issued from his ears;
He prays to God that He will call the peers,
Bids Gabriel, the angel, t' himself appear.
Takes the olifant, that no reproach shall hear,
And Durendal in the other hand he wields;
Further than might a cross-bow's arrow speed
Goes towards Spain into a fallow-field;
Climbs on a cliff; where, under two fair trees,
Four terraces, of marble wrought, he sees.
There he falls down, and lies upon the green;
He swoons again, for death is very near.

CLXIX

High are the peaks, the trees are very high.
Four terraces of polished marble shine;
On the green grass count Rollant swoons thereby.
A Sarrazin him all the time espies,
Who feigning death among the others hides;
Blood hath his face and all his body dyed;
He gets afoot, running towards him hies;
Fair was he, strong and of a courage high;
A mortal hate he's kindled in his pride.
He's seized Rollant, and the arms, were at his side,

"Charlè's nephew," he's said, "here conquered lies.
To Araby I'll bear this sword as prize."
As he drew it, something the count descried.

CLXX

So Rollant felt his sword was taken forth,
Opened his eyes, and this word to him spoke:
"Thou'rt never one of ours, full well I know."
Took the olifant, that he would not let go,
Struck him on th' helm, that jewelled was with gold,
And broke its steel, his skull and all his bones,
Out of his head both the two eyes he drove;
Dead at his feet he has the pagan thrown:
After he's said: "Culvert, thou wert too bold,
Or right or wrong, of my sword seizing hold!
They'll dub thee fool, to whom the tale is told.
But my great one, my olifant I broke;
Fallen from it the crystal and the gold."

CLXXI

Then Rollant feels that he has lost his sight,
Climbs to his feet, uses what strength he might;
In all his face the colour is grown white.
In front of him a great brown boulder lies;
Whereon ten blows with grief and rage he strikes;
The steel cries out, but does not break outright;
And the count says: "Saint Mary, be my guide!
Good Durendal, unlucky is your plight!
I've need of you no more; spent is my pride!
We in the field have won so many fights,
Combating through so many regions wide
That Charlès holds, whose beard is hoary white!
Be you not his that turns from any in flight!
A good vassal has held you this long time;
Never shall France the Free behold his like."

CLXXII

Rollant hath struck the sardonyx terraçe;
The steel cries out, but broken is no ways.
So when he sees he never can it break,
Within himself begins he to complain:
"Ah! Durendal, white art thou, clear of stain!
Beneath the sun reflecting back his rays!
In Moriane was Charlès, in the vale,
When from heaven God by His angel bade
Him give thee to a count and capitain;
Girt thee on me that noble King and great.
I won for him with thee Anjou, Bretaigne,
And won for him with thee Peitou, the Maine,
And Normandy the free for him I gained,
Also with thee Provence and Equitaigne,
And Lumbardie and all the whole Romaigne,
I won Baivere, all Flanders in the plain,
Also Burguigne and all the whole Puillane,
Costentinnople, that homage to him pays;
In Saisonie all is as he ordains;
With thee I won him Scotland, Ireland, Wales,
England also, where he his chamber makes;
Won I with thee so many countries strange
That Charlès holds, whose beard is white with age!
For this sword's sake sorrow upon me weighs,
Rather I'ld die, than it mid pagans stay.
Lord God Father, never let France be shamed!"

CLXXIII

Rollant his stroke on a dark stone repeats,
And more of it breaks off than I can speak.
The sword cries out, yet breaks not in the least,
Back from the blow into the air it leaps.
Destroy it can he not; which when he sees,

Within himself he makes a plaint most sweet:
"Ah! Durendal, most holy, fair indeed!
Relics enough thy golden hilt conceals:
Saint Peter's Tooth, the Blood of Saint Basile,
Some of the Hairs of my Lord, Saint Denise,
Some of the Robe, was worn by Saint Mary.
It is not right that pagans should thee seize,
For Christian men your use shall ever be.
Nor any man's that worketh cowardice!
Many broad lands with you have I retrieved
Which Charlès holds, who hath the great white beard;
Wherefore that King so proud and rich is he."

CLXXIV

But Rollant felt that death had made a way
Down from his head till on his heart it lay;
Beneath a pine running in haste he came,
On the green grass he lay there on his face;
His olifant and sword beneath him placed,
Turning his head towards the pagan race,
Now this he did, in truth, that Charles might say
(As he desired) and all the Franks his race:
'Ah, gentle count; conquering he was slain!'
He owned his faults often and every way,
And for his sins his glove to God upraised. AOI.

CLXXV

But Rollant feels he's no more time to seek;
Looking to Spain, he lies on a sharp peak,
And with one hand upon his breast he beats:
"*Mea Culpa!* God, by Thy Virtues clean
Me from my sins, the mortal and the mean,
Which from the hour that I was born have been
Until this day, when life is ended here!"
Holds out his glove towards God, as he speaks;

Angels descend from heaven on that scene. AOI.

CLXXVI

The count Rollant, beneath a pine he sits;
Turning his eyes towards Spain, he begins
Remembering so many divers things:
So many lands where he went conquering,
And France the Douce, the heroes of his kin,
And Charlemagne, his lord who nourished him.
Nor can he help but weep and sigh at this.
But his own self, he's not forgotten him,
He owns his faults, and God's forgiveness bids:
"Very Father, in Whom no falsehood is,
Saint Lazaron from death Thou didst remit,
And Daniel save from the lions' pit;
My soul in me preserve from all perils
And from the sins I did in life commit!"
His right-hand glove, to God he offers it
Saint Gabriel from 's hand hath taken it.
Over his arm his head bows down and slips,
He joins his hands: and so is life finish'd.
God sent him down His angel cherubin,
And Saint Michael, we worship in peril;
And by their side Saint Gabriel alit;
So the count's soul they bare to Paradis.

CLXXVII

Rollant is dead; his soul to heav'n God bare.
That Emperour to Rencesvals doth fare.
There was no path nor passage anywhere,
Nor of waste ground no ell nor foot to spare
Without a Frank or pagan lying there.
Charles cries aloud: "Where are you, nephew fair?
Where's the Archbishop and that count Oliviers?
Where is Gerins and his comrade Gerers?
Otès the Duke, and the count Berengiers
And Ivorie, and Ive, so dear they were?
What is become of Gascon Engelier,
Sansun the Duke and Anséis the fierce?
Where's old Gerard of Russillun; oh, where
The dozen peers I left behind me here?"
But what avail, since none can answer bear?

"God!" says the King, "Now well may I despair,
I was not here the first assault to share!"
Seeming enraged, his beard the King doth tear.
Weep from their eyes barons and chevaliers,
A thousand score, they swoon upon the earth;
Duke Neimes for them was moved with pity rare.

CLXXVIII

No chevalier nor baron is there, who
Pitifully weeps not for grief and dule;
They mourn their sons, their brothers, their nephews,
And their liege lords, and trusty friends and true;
Upon the ground a many of them swoon.
Thereon Duke Neimes doth act with wisdom proof,
First before all he's said to the Emperour:
"See beforehand, a league from us or two,
From the highways dust rising in our view;
Pagans are there, and many of them, too.
Canter therefore! Vengeance upon them do!"
"Ah, God!" says Charles, "so far are they removed!
Do right by me, my honour still renew!
They've torn from me the flower of France the Douce."
The King commands Gebuin and Otun,
Tedbalt of Reims, also the count Milun:
"Guard me this field, these hills and valleys too,
Let the dead lie, all as they are, unmoved,
Let not approach lion, nor any brute;
Let not approach esquire, nor any groom;
For I forbid that any come thereto,
Until God will that we return anew."
These answer him sweetly, their love to prove:
"Right Emperour, dear Sire, so will we do."
A thousand knights they keep in retinue. AOI.

CLXXIX

That Emperour bids trumpets sound again,
Then canters forth with his great host so brave.
Of Spanish men, whose backs are turned their way,
Franks one and all continue in their chase.
When the King sees the light at even fade,
On the green grass dismounting as he may,
He kneels aground, to God the Lord doth pray
That the sun's course He will for him delay,
Put off the night, and still prolong the day.
An angel then, with him should reason make,
Nimbly enough appeared to him and spake:
"Charles, canter on! Light needst not thou await.
The flower of France, as God knows well, is slain;
Thou canst be avenged upon that crimeful race."
Upon that word mounts the Emperour again. AOI.

CLXXX

For Charlemagne a great marvel God planned:
Making the sun still in his course to stand.
So pagans fled, and chased them well the Franks
Through the Valley of Shadows, close in hand;
Towards Sarraguce by force they chased them back,
And as they went with killing blows attacked:
Barred their highways and every path they had.
The River Sebre before them reared its bank,
'Twas very deep, marvellous current ran;
No barge thereon nor dromond nor caland.
A god of theirs invoked they, Tervagant.
And then leaped in, but there no warrant had.
The armèd men more weighty were for that,
Many of them down to the bottom sank,
Downstream the rest floated as they might hap;
So much water the luckiest of them drank,

That all were drowned, with marvellous keen pangs.
"An evil day," cry Franks, "ye saw Rollant!"

CLXXXI

When Charlès sees that pagans all are dead,
Some of them slain, the greater part drownèd;
(Whereby great spoils his chevaliers collect)
That gentle King upon his feet descends,
Kneels on the ground, his thanks to God presents.
When he once more rises, the sun is set.
Says the Emperour: "Time is to pitch our tents;
To Rencesvals too late to go again.
Our horses are worn out and founderèd:
Unsaddle them, take bridles from their heads,
And through these meads let them refreshment get."
Answer the Franks: "Sire, you have spoken well." AOI.

CLXXXII

That Emperour hath chosen his bivouac;
The Franks dismount in those deserted tracts,
Their saddles take from off their horses' backs,
Bridles of gold from off their heads unstrap,
Let them go free; there is enough fresh grass—
No service can they render them, save that.
Who is most tired sleeps on the ground stretched flat.
Upon this night no sentinels keep watch.

CLXXXIII

That Emperour is lying in a mead;
By's head, so brave, he's placed his mighty spear;
On such a night unarmed he will not be.
He's donned his white hauberk, with broidery,
Has laced his helm, jewelled with golden beads,
Girt on Joiuse, there never was its peer,
Whereon each day thirty fresh hues appear.
All of us know that lance, and well may speak

Whereby Our Lord was wounded on the Tree.
Charles, by God's grace, possessed its point of steel!
His golden hilt he enshrined it underneath.
By that honour and by that sanctity
The name Joiuse was for that sword decreed.
Barons of France may not forgetful be
Whence comes the ensign "Monjoie," they cry at need;
Wherefore no race against them can succeed.

CLXXXIV

Clear was the night, the moon shone radiant.
Charles laid him down, but sorrow for Rollant
And Oliver, most heavy on him he had,
For 's dozen peers, for all the Frankish band
He had left dead in bloody Rencesvals;
He could not help, but wept and waxèd mad,
And prayed to God to be their souls' warrant.
Weary that King, for grief he's very sad;
He falls on sleep, he can no more withstand.
Through all those meads they slumber then, the Franks;
Is not a horse can any longer stand,
Who would eat grass, he takes it lying flat.
He has learned much, can understand their pangs.

CLXXXV

Charles, like a man worn out with labour, slept.
Saint Gabriel the Lord to him hath sent,
Whom as a guard o'er the Emperour he set;
Stood all night long that angel by his head.
In a vision announcèd he to him then
A battle, should be fought against him yet,
Significance of griefs demonstrated.
Charlès looked up towards the sky, and there
Thunders and winds and blowing gales beheld,
And hurricanes and marvellous tempests;

Lightnings and flames he saw in readiness,
That speedily on all his people fell;
Apple and ash, their spear-shafts all burnèd,
Also their shields, e'en the golden bosses,
Crumbled the shafts of their trenchant lances,
Crushed their hauberks and all their steel helmets.
His chevaliers he saw in great distress.
Bears and leopards would feed upon them next;
Adversaries, dragons, wyverns, serpents,
Griffins were there, thirty thousand, no less,
Nor was there one but on some Frank it set.
And the Franks cried: "Ah! Charlemagne, give help!"
Wherefore the King much grief and pity felt,
He'ld go to them but was in duress kept:
Out of a wood came a great lion then,
'Twas very proud and fierce and terrible;
His body dear sought out, and on him leapt,
Each in his arms, wrestling, the other held;
But he knew not which conquered, nor which fell.
That Emperour woke not at all, but slept.

CLXXXVI

And, after that, another vision came:
Himseemed in France, at Aix, on a terrace,
And that he held a bruin by two chains;
Out of Ardenne saw thirty bears that came,
And each of them words, as a man might, spake:
Said to him: "Sire, give him to us again!
It is not right that he with you remain,
He's of our kin, and we must lend him aid."
A harrier fair ran out of his palace,
Among them all the greatest bear assailed
On the green grass, beyond his friends some way.
There saw the King marvellous give and take;

But he knew not which fell, nor which o'ercame.
The angel of God so much to him made plain.
Charlès slept on till the clear dawn of day.

CLXXXVII

King Marsilies, fleeing to Sarraguce,
Dismounted there beneath an olive cool;
His sword and sark and helm aside he put,
On the green grass lay down in shame and gloom;
For his right hand he'd lost, 'was clean cut through;
Such blood he'd shed, in anguish keen he swooned.
Before his face his lady Bramimunde
Bewailed and cried, with very bitter rue;
Twenty thousand and more around him stood,
All of them cursed Carlun and France the Douce.
Then Apollin in's grotto they surround,
And threaten him, and ugly words pronounce:
"Such shame on us, vile god, why bringest thou?
This is our king: wherefore dost him confound?
Who served thee oft, ill recompense hath found."
Then they take off his sceptre and his crown,
With their hands hang him from a column down,
Among their feet trample him on the ground,
With great cudgels they batter him and trounce.
From Tervagant his carbuncle they impound,
And Mahumet into a ditch fling out,
Where swine and dogs defile him and devour.

CLXXXVIII

Out of his swoon awakens Marsilies,
And has him borne his vaulted roof beneath;
Many colours were painted there to see,
And Bramimunde laments for him, the queen,
Tearing her hair; caitiff herself she clepes;
Also these words cries very loud and clear:

"Ah! Sarraguce, henceforth forlorn thou'lt be
Of the fair king that had thee in his keep!
All those our gods have wrought great felony,
Who in battle this morning failed at need.
That admiral will shew his cowardice,
Unless he fight against that race hardy,
Who are so fierce, for life they take no heed.
That Emperour, with his blossoming beard,
Hath vassalage, and very high folly;
Battle to fight, he will not ever flee.
Great grief it is, no man may slay him clean."

CLXXXIX

That Emperour, by his great Majesty,
Full seven years in Spain now has he been,
And castles there, and many cities seized.
King Marsilies was therefore sore displeased;
In the first year he sealed and sent his brief
To Baligant, into Babilonie:
('Twas the admiral, old in antiquity,
That clean outlived Omer and Virgilie,)
To Sarraguce, with succour bade him speed,
For, if he failed, Marsile his gods would leave,
All his idols he worshipped formerly;
He would receive blest Christianity
And reconciled to Charlemagne would be.
Long time that one came not, far off was he.
Through forty realms he did his tribes rally;
His great dromonds, he made them all ready,
Barges and skiffs and ships and galleries;
Neath Alexandre, a haven next the sea,
In readiness he gat his whole navy.
That was in May, first summer of the year,
All of his hosts he launched upon the sea.

CXC

Great are the hosts of that opposèd race;
With speed they sail, they steer and navigate.
High on their yards, at their mast-heads they place
Lanterns enough, and carbuncles so great
Thence, from above, such light they dissipate
The sea's more clear at midnight than by day.
And when they come into the land of Spain
All that country lightens and shines again:
Of their coming Marsile has heard the tale. AOI.

CXCI

The pagan race would never rest, but come
Out of the sea, where the sweet waters run;
They leave Marbris, they leave behind Marbrus,
Upstream by Sebre doth all their navy turn.
Lanterns they have, and carbuncles enough,
That all night long and very clearly burn.
Upon that day they come to Sarragus. AOI.

CXCII

Clear is that day and the sun radiant.
Out of his barge issues their admiral,
Espaneliz goes forth at his right hand,
Seventeen kings follow him in a band,
Counts too, and dukes; I cannot tell of that.
Where in a field, midway, a laurel stands,
On the green grass they spread a white silk mat,
Set a fald-stool there, made of olifant;
Sits him thereon the pagan Baligant,
And all the rest in rows about him stand.
The lord of them speaks before any man:
"Listen to me, free knights and valiant!
Charlès the King, the Emperour of the Franks,
Shall not eat bread, save when that I command.

Throughout all Spain great war with me he's had;
I will go seek him now, into Douce France,
I will not cease, while I'm a living man,
Till he be slain, or fall between my hands."
Upon his knee his right-hand glove he slaps.

CXCIII

He is fast bound by all that he has said.
He will not fail, for all the gold neath heav'n,
But go to Aix, where Charlè's court is held:
His men applaud, for so they counsellèd.
After he called two of his chevaliers,
One Clarifan, and the other Clarïen:
"You are the sons of king Maltraïen,
Freely was wont my messages to bear.
You I command to Sarraguce to fare.
Marsiliun on my part you shall tell
Against the Franks I'm come to give him help,
Find I their host, great battle shall be there;
Give him this glove, that's stitched with golden thread,
On his right hand let it be worn and held;
This little wand of fine gold take as well,
Bid him come here, his homage to declare.
To France I'll go, and war with Charles again;
Save at my feet he kneel, and mercy beg,
Save all the laws of Christians he forget,
I'll take away the crown from off his head."
Answer pagans: "Sire, you say very well."

CXCIV

Said Baligant: "But canter now, barons,
Take one the wand, and the other one the glove!"
These answer him: "Dear lord, it shall be done."
Canter so far, to Sarraguce they come,
Pass through ten gates, across four bridges run,

Through all the streets wherein the burghers crowd.
When they draw nigh the citadel above,
From the palace they hear a mighty sound;
About that place are seen pagans enough,
Who weep and cry, with grief are waxen wood,
And curse their gods, Tervagan and Mahum
And Apolin, from whom no help is come.
Says each to each: "Caitiffs! What shall be done?
For upon us confusion vile is come,
Now have we lost our king Marsiliun,
For yesterday his hand count Rollant cut;
We'll have no more Fair Jursaleu, his son;
The whole of Spain henceforward is undone."
Both messengers on the terrace dismount.

CXCV

Horses they leave under an olive tree,
Which by the reins two Sarrazins do lead;
Those messengers have wrapped them in their weeds,
To the palace they climb the topmost steep.
When they're come in, the vaulted roof beneath,
Marsilium with courtesy they greet:
"May Mahumet, who all of us doth keep,
And Tervagan, and our lord Apoline
Preserve the king and guard from harm the queen!"
Says Bramimunde: "Great foolishness I hear:
Those gods of ours in cowardice are steeped;
In Rencesvals they wrought an evil deed,
Our chevaliers they let be slain in heaps;
My lord they failed in battle, in his need,
Never again will he his right hand see;
For that rich count, Rollant, hath made him bleed.
All our whole Spain shall be for Charles to keep.
Miserable! What shall become of me?

Alas! That I've no man to slay me clean!" AOI.

CXCVI

Says Clarïen: "My lady, say not that!
We're messengers from pagan Baligant;
To Marsilies, he says, he'll be warrant,
So sends him here his glove, also this wand.
Vessels we have, are moored by Sebrè's bank,
Barges and skiffs and gallies four thousand,
Dromonds are there—I cannot speak of that.
Our admiral is wealthy and puissant.
And Charlemagne he will go seek through France
And quittance give him, dead or recreant."
Says Bramimunde: "Unlucky journey, that!
Far nearer here you'll light upon the Franks;
For seven years he's stayed now in this land.
That Emperour is bold and combatant,
Rather he'ld die than from the field draw back;
No king neath heav'n above a child he ranks.
Charles hath no fear for any living man."

CXCVII

Says Marsilies the king: "Now let that be."
To th' messengers: "Sirs, pray you, speak to me.
I am held fast by death, as ye may see.
No son have I nor daughter to succeed;
That one I had, they slew him yester-eve.
Bid you my lord, he come to see me here.
Rights over Spain that admiral hath he,
My claim to him, if he will take 't, I yield;
But from the Franks he then must set her free.
Gainst Charlemagne I'll shew him strategy:
Within a month from now he'll conquered be.
Of Sarraguce ye'll carry him the keys,
He'll go not hence, say, if he trusts in me."

They answer him: "Sir, 'tis the truth you speak." AOI.

CXCVIII

Then says Marsile: "The Emperour, Charles the Great
Hath slain my men and all my land laid waste,
My cities are broken and violate;
He lay this night upon the river Sebre;
I've counted well, 'tis seven leagues away.
Bid the admiral, leading his host this way,
Do battle here; this word to him convey."
Gives them the keys of Sarraguce her gates;
Both messengers their leave of him do take,
Upon that word bow down, and turn away.

CXCIX

Both messengers did on their horses mount;
From that city nimbly they issued out.
Then, sore afraid, their admiral they sought,
To whom the keys of Sarraguce they brought.
Says Baligant: "Speak now; what have ye found?
Where's Marsilies, to come to me was bound?"
Says Clarïen: "To death he's stricken down.
That Emperour was in the pass but now;
To France the Douce he would be homeward-bound,
Rereward he set, to save his great honour:
His nephew there installed, Rollant the count,
And Oliver; the dozen peers around;
A thousand score of Franks in armour found.
Marsile the king fought with them there, so proud;
He and Rollant upon that field did joust.
With Durendal he dealt him such a clout
From his body he cut the right hand down.
His son is dead, in whom his heart was bound,
And the barons that service to him vowed;
Fleeing he came, he could no more hold out.

That Emperour has chased him well enow.
The king implores, you'll hasten with succour,
Yields to you Spain, his kingdom and his crown."
And Baligant begins to think, and frowns;
Such grief he has, doth nearly him confound. AOI.

CC

"Sir admiral," said to him Clarïens,
"In Rencesvals was yesterday battle.
Dead is Rollant and that count Oliver,
The dozen peers whom Charle so cherishèd,
And of their Franks are twenty thousand dead.
King Marsilie's of his right hand bereft,
And the Emperour chased him enow from thence.
Throughout this land no chevalier is left,
But he be slain, or drowned in Sebrè's bed.
By river side the Franks have pitched their tents,
Into this land so near to us they've crept;
But, if you will, grief shall go with them hence."
And Baligant looked on him proudly then,
In his courage grew joyous and content;
From the fald-stool upon his feet he leapt,
Then cried aloud: "Barons, too long ye've slept;
Forth from your ships issue, mount, canter well!
If he flee not, that Charlemagne the eld,
King Marsilies shall somehow be avenged;
For his right hand I'll pay him back an head."

CCI

Pagan Arabs out of their ships issue,
Then mount upon their horses and their mules,
And canter forth, (nay, what more might they do?)
Their admiral, by whom they all were ruled,
Called up to him Gemalfin, whom he knew:
"I give command of all my hosts to you."

On a brown horse mounted, as he was used,
And in his train he took with him four dukes.
Cantered so far, he came to Sarraguce.
Dismounted on a floor of marble blue,
Where four counts were, who by his stirrup stood;
Up by the steps, the palace came into;
To meet him there came running Bramimunde,
Who said to him: "Accursèd from the womb,
That in such shame my sovran lord I lose!
Fell at his feet, that admiral her took.
In grief they came up into Marsile's room. AOI.

CCII

King Marsilies, when he sees Baligant,
Calls to him then two Spanish Sarazands:
"Take me by the arms, and so lift up my back."
One of his gloves he takes in his left hand;
Then says Marsile: "Sire, king and admiral,
Quittance I give you here of all my land,
With Sarraguce, and the honour thereto hangs.
Myself I've lost; my army, every man."
He answers him: "Therefore the more I'm sad.
No long discourse together may we have;
Full well I know, Charles waits not our attack,
I take the glove from you, in spite of that."
He turned away in tears, such grief he had.
Down by the steps, out of the palace ran,
Mounted his horse, to 's people gallopped back.
Cantered so far, he came before his band;
From hour to hour then, as he went, he sang:
"Pagans, come on: already flee the Franks!" AOI.

CCIII

In morning time, when the dawn breaks at last,
Awakenèd is that Emperour Charles.

Saint Gabriel, who on God's part him guards,
Raises his hand, the Sign upon him marks.
Rises the King, his arms aside he's cast,
The others then, through all the host, disarm.
After they mount, by virtue canter fast
Through those long ways and through those roads so large;
They go to see the marvellous damage
In Rencesvals, there where the battle was. AOI.

CCIV

In Rencesvals is Charlès enterèd,
Begins to weep for those he finds there dead;
Says to the Franks: "My lords, restrain your steps,
Since I myself alone should go ahead,
For my nephew, whom I would find again.
At Aix I was, upon the feast Noel,
Vaunted them there my valiant chevaliers,
Of battles great and very hot contests;
With reason thus I heard Rollant speak then:
He would not die in any foreign realm
Ere he'd surpassed his peers and all his men.
To the foes' land he would have turned his head,
Conqueringly his gallant life he'ld end."
Further than one a little wand could send,
Before the rest he's on a peak mounted.

CCV

When the Emperour went seeking his nephew,
He found the grass, and every flower that bloomed,
Turned scarlat, with our barons' blood imbrued;
Pity he felt, he could but weep for rue.
Beneath two trees he climbed the hill and looked,
And Rollant's strokes on three terraces knew,
On the green grass saw lying his nephew;
'Tis nothing strange that Charlè's anger grew.

Dismounted then, and went—his heart was full,
In his two hands the count's body he took;
With anguish keen he fell on him and swooned.

CCVI

That Emperour is from his swoon revived.
Naimès the Duke, and the count Aceline,
Gefrei d'Anjou and his brother Tierry,
Take up the King, bear him beneath a pine.
There on the ground he sees his nephew lie.
Most sweetly then begins he to repine:
"Rollant, my friend, may God to thee be kind!
Never beheld any man such a knight
So to engage and so to end a fight.
Now my honour is turned into decline!"
Charle swoons again, he cannot stand upright. AOI.

CCVII

Charlès the King returned out of his swoon.
Him in their hands four of his barons took,
He looked to the earth, saw lying his nephew;
All colourless his lusty body grew,
He turned his eyes, were very shadowful.
Charlès complained in amity and truth:
"Rollant, my friend, God lay thee mid the blooms
Of Paradise, among the glorious!
Thou cam'st to Spain in evil tide, seigneur!
Day shall not dawn, for thee I've no dolour.
How perishes my strength and my valour!
None shall I have now to sustain my honour;
I think I've not one friend neath heaven's roof,
Kinsmen I have, but none of them's so proof."
He tore his locks, till both his hands were full.
Five score thousand Franks had such great dolour
There was not one but sorely wept for rue. AOI.

CCVIII

"Rollant, my friend, to France I will away;
When at Loüm, I'm in my hall again,
Strange men will come from many far domains,
Who'll ask me, where's that count, the Capitain;
I'll say to them that he is dead in Spain.
In bitter grief henceforward shall I reign,
Day shall not dawn, I weep not nor complain.

CCIX

"Rollant, my friend, fair youth that bar'st the bell,
When I arrive at Aix, in my Chapelle,
Men coming there will ask what news I tell;
I'll say to them: 'Marvellous news and fell.
My nephew's dead, who won for me such realms!"
Against me then the Saxon will rebel,
Hungar, Bulgar, and many hostile men,
Romain, Puillain, all those are in Palerne,
And in Affrike, and those in Califerne;
Afresh then will my pain and suffrance swell.
For who will lead my armies with such strength,
When he is slain, that all our days us led?
Ah! France the Douce, now art thou deserted!
Such grief I have that I would fain be dead."
All his white beard he hath begun to rend,
Tore with both hands the hair out of his head.
Five score thousand Franks swooned on the earth and fell

CCX

"Rollant, my friend, God shew thee His mercy!
In Paradise repose the soul of thee!
Who hath thee slain, exile for France decreed.
I'ld live no more, so bitter is my grief
For my household, who have been slain for me.
God grant me this, the Son of Saint Mary,

Ere I am come to th' master-pass of Size,
From my body my soul at length go free!
Among their souls let mine in glory be,
And let my flesh upon their flesh be heaped."
Still his white beard he tears, and his eyes weep.
Duke Naimès says: "His wrath is great indeed." AOI.

CCXI

"Sire, Emperour," Gefrei d'Anjou implored,
"Let not your grief to such excess be wrought;
Bid that our men through all this field be sought,
Whom those of Spain have in the battle caught;
In a charnel command that they be borne."
Answered the King: "Sound then upon your horn." AOI.

CCXII

Gefrei d'Anjou upon his trumpet sounds;
As Charlès bade them, all the Franks dismount.
All of their friends, whose bodies they have found
To a charnel speedily they bring down.
Bishops there are, and abbots there enow,
Canons and monks, vicars with shaven crowns;
Absolution in God's name they've pronounced;
Incense and myrrh with precious gums they've ground,
And lustily they've swung the censers round;
With honour great they've laid them in the ground.
They've left them there; what else might they do now?
AOI.

CCXIII

That Emperour sets Rollant on one side
And Oliver, and the Archbishop Turpin;
Their bodies bids open before his eyes
And all their hearts in silken veils to wind,
And set them in coffers of marble white;
After, they take the bodies of those knights,

Each of the three is wrapped in a deer's hide;
They're washen well in allspice and in wine.
The King commands Tedbalt and Gebuin,
Marquis Otun, Milun the count besides:
Along the road in three wagons to drive.
They're covered well with carpets Galazine. AOI.

CCXIV

Now to be off would that Emperour Charles,
When pagans, lo! comes surging the vanguard;
Two messengers come from their ranks forward,
From the admiral bring challenge to combat:
"'Tis not yet time, proud King, that thou depart.
Lo, Baligant comes cantering afterward,
Great are the hosts he leads from Arab parts;
This day we'll see if thou hast vassalage."
Charlès the King his snowy beard has clasped,
Remembering his sorrow and damage,
Haughtily then his people all regards,
In a loud voice he cries with all his heart:
"Barons and Franks, to horse, I say, to arms!" AOI.

CCXV

First before all was armed that Emperour,
Nimbly enough his iron sark indued,
Laced up his helm, girt on his sword Joiuse,
Outshone the sun that dazzling light it threw,
Hung from his neck a shield, was of Girunde,
And took his spear, was fashioned at Blandune.
On his good horse then mounted, Tencendur,
Which he had won at th' ford below Marsune
When he flung dead Malpalin of Nerbune,
Let go the reins, spurred him with either foot;
Five score thousand behind him as he flew,
Calling on God and the Apostle of Roum. AOI.

CCXVI

Through all the field dismount the Frankish men,
Five-score thousand and more, they arm themselves;
The gear they have enhances much their strength,
Their horses swift, their arms are fashioned well;
Mounted they are, and fight with great science.
Find they that host, battle they'll render them.
Their gonfalons flutter above their helms.
When Charlès sees the fair aspect of them,
He calls to him Jozeran of Provence,
Naimon the Duke, with Antelme of Maience:
"In such vassals should man have confidence,
Whom not to trust were surely want of sense;
Unless the Arabs of coming here repent,
Then Rollant's life, I think, we'll dearly sell."
Answers Duke Neimes: "God grant us his consent!"

CCXVII AOI.

Charlès hath called Rabel and Guineman;
Thus said the King: "My lords, you I command
To take their place, Olivier and Rollant,
One bear the sword and the other the olifant;
So canter forth ahead, before the van,
And in your train take fifteen thousand Franks,
Young bachelors, that are most valiant.
As many more shall after them advance,
Whom Gebuins shall lead, also Lorains."
Naimès the Duke and the count Jozerans
Go to adjust these columns in their ranks.
Find they that host, they'll make a grand attack. AOI.

CCXVIII

Of Franks the first columns made ready there,
After those two a third they next prepare;
In it are set the vassals of Baiviere,

Some thousand score high-prizèd chevaliers;
Never was lost the battle, where they were;
Charles for no race neath heaven hath more care,
Save those of France, who realms for him conquered.
The Danish chief, the warrior count Oger,
Shall lead that troop, for haughty is their air. AOI.

CCXIX

Three columns now, he has, the Emperour Charles.
Naimes the Duke a fourth next sets apart
Of good barons, endowed with vassalage;
Germans they are, come from the German March,
A thousand score, as all said afterward;
They're well equipped with horses and with arms,
Rather they'll die than from the battle pass;
They shall be led by Hermans, Duke of Trace,
Who'll die before he's any way coward. AOI.

CCXX

Naimès the Duke and the count Jozerans
The fifth column have mustered, of Normans,
A thousand score, or so say all the Franks;
Well armed are they, their horses charge and prance;
Rather they'ld die, than e'er be recreant;
No race neath heav'n can more in th' field compass.
Richard the old, lead them in th' field he shall,
He'll strike hard there with his good trenchant lance.

CCXXI AOI.

The sixth column is mustered of Bretons;
Thirty thousand chevaliers therein come;
These canter in the manner of barons,
Upright their spears, their ensigns fastened on.
The overlord of them is named Oedon,
Who doth command the county Nevelon,
Tedbald of Reims and the marquis Oton:

"Lead ye my men, by my commission." AOI.

CCXXII

That Emperour hath now six columns yare
Naimès the Duke the seventh next prepares
Of Peitevins and barons from Alverne;
Forty thousand chevaliers might be there;
Their horses good, their arms are all most fair.
They're neath a cliff, in a vale by themselves;
With his right hand King Charlès hath them blessed,
Them Jozerans shall lead, also Godselmes. AOI.

CCXXIII

And the eighth column hath Naimès made ready;
'Tis of Flamengs, and barons out of Frise;
Forty thousand and more good knights are these,
Nor lost by them has any battle been.
And the King says: "These shall do my service."
Between Rembalt and Hamon of Galice
Shall they be led, for all their chivalry. AOI.

CCXXIV

Between Naimon and Jozeran the count
Are prudent men for the ninth column found,
Of Lotherengs and those out of Borgoune;
Fifty thousand good knights they are, by count;
In helmets laced and sarks of iron brown,
Strong are their spears, short are the shafts cut down.
If the Arrabits demur not, but come out
And trust themselves to these, they'll strike them down.
Tierris the Duke shall lead them, of Argoune. AOI.

CCXXV

The tenth column is of Barons of France,
Five score thousand of our best capitans;
Lusty of limb, and proud of countenance,
Snowy their heads are, and their beards are blanched,

In doubled sarks, and in hauberks they're clad,
Girt on their sides Frankish and Spanish brands
And noble shields of divers cognisance.
Soon as they mount, the battle they demand,
"Monjoie" they cry. With them goes Charlemagne.
Gefrei d'Anjou carries that oriflamme;
Saint Peter's 'twas, and bare the name Roman,
But on that day Monjoie, by change, it gat. AOI.

CCXXVI

That Emperour down from his horse descends;
To the green grass, kneeling, his face he bends.
Then turns his eyes towards the Orient,
Calls upon God with heartiest intent:
"Very Father, this day do me defend,
Who to Jonas succour didst truly send
Out of the whale's belly, where he was pent;
And who didst spare the king of Niniven,
And Daniel from marvellous torment
When he was caged within the lions' den;
And three children, all in a fire ardent:
Thy gracious Love to me be here present.
In Thy Mercy, if it please Thee, consent
That my nephew Rollant I may avenge."
When he had prayed, upon his feet he stepped,
With the strong mark of virtue signed his head;
Upon his swift charger the King mounted
While Jozerans and Neimes his stirrup held;
He took his shield, his trenchant spear he kept;
Fine limbs he had, both gallant and well set;
Clear was his face and filled with good intent.
Vigorously he cantered onward thence.
In front, in rear, they sounded their trumpets,
Above them all boomed the olifant again.

Then all the Franks for pity of Rollant wept.

CCXXVII

That Emperour canters in noble array,
Over his sark all of his beard displays;
For love of him, all others do the same,
Five score thousand Franks are thereby made plain.
They pass those peaks, those rocks and those mountains,
Those terrible narrows, and those deep vales,
Then issue from the passes and the wastes
Till they are come into the March of Spain;
A halt they've made, in th' middle of a plain.
To Baligant his vanguard comes again
A Sulian hath told him his message:
"We have seen Charles, that haughty sovereign;
Fierce are his men, they have no mind to fail.
Arm yourself then: battle you'll have to-day."
Says Baligant: "Mine is great vassalage;
Let horns this news to my pagans proclaim."

CCXXVIII

Through all the host they have their drums sounded,
And their bugles, and very clear trumpets.
Pagans dismount, that they may arm themselves.
Their admiral will stay no longer then;
Puts on a sark, embroidered in the hems,
Laces his helm that is with gold begemmed;
After, his sword on his left side he's set,
Out of his pride a name for it he's spelt
Like to Carlun's, as he has heard it said,
So Preciuse he bad his own be clept;
'Twas their ensign when they to battle went,
His chevaliers'; he gave that cry to them.
His own broad shield he hangs upon his neck,
(Round its gold boss a band of crystal went,

The strap of it was a good silken web;)
He grasps his spear, the which he calls Maltet—
So great its shaft as is a stout cudgel,
Beneath its steel alone, a mule had bent.
On his charger is Baligant mounted,
Marcules, from over seas, his stirrup held.
That warrior, with a great stride he stepped,
Small were his thighs, his ribs of wide extent,
Great was his breast, and finely fashionèd,
With shoulders broad and very clear aspect;
Proud was his face, his hair was ringleted,
White as a flow'r in summer was his head.
His vassalage had often been provèd.
God! what a knight, were he a Christian yet!
His horse he's spurred, the clear blood issuèd;
He's gallopped on, over a ditch he's leapt,
Full fifty feet a man might mark its breadth.
Pagans cry out: "Our Marches shall be held;
There is no Frank, may once with him contest,
Will he or nill, his life he'll soon have spent.
Charlès is mad, that he departs not hence."   AOI.

CCXXIX

That admiral to a baron's like enough,
White is his beard as flowers by summer burnt;
In his own laws, of wisdom hath he much;
And in battle he's proud and arduous.
His son Malprimes is very chivalrous,
He's great and strong;—his ancestors were thus.
Says to his sire: "To canter then let us!
I marvel much that soon we'll see Carlun."
Says Baligant: "Yea, for he's very pruff;
In many tales honour to him is done;
He hath no more Rollant, his sister's son,

He'll have no strength to stay in fight with us." AOI.

CCXXX

"Fair son Malprimes," then says t' him Baligant,
"Was slain yestre'en the good vassal Rollant,
And Oliver, the proof and valiant,
The dozen peers, whom Charles so cherished, and
Twenty thousand more Frankish combatants.
For all the rest I'ld not unglove my hand.
But the Emperour is verily come back,
—So tells me now my man, that Sulian—
Ten great columns, he's set them in their ranks;
He's a proof man who sounds that olifant,
With a clear call he rallies his comrades;
These at the head come cantering in advance,
Also with them are fifteen thousand Franks,
Young bachelors whom Charlès calls Infants;
As many again come following that band,
Who will lay on with utmost arrogance."
Then says Malprimes: "The first blow I demand." AOI.

CCXXXI

"Fair son Malprimes," says Baligant to him,
"I grant it you, as you have asked me this;
Against the Franks go now, and smite them quick.
And take with you Torleu, the Persian king
And Dapamort, another king Leutish.
Their arrogance if you can humble it,
Of my domains a slice to you I'll give
From Cheriant unto the Vale Marquis."
"I thank you, Sire!" Malprimes answers him;
Going before, he takes delivery;
'Tis of that land, was held by king Flurit.
After that hour he never looked on it,
Investiture gat never, nor seizin.

CCXXXII

That admiral canters among his hosts;
After, his son with's great body follows,
Torleus the king, and the king Dapamort;
Thirty columns most speedily they form.
They've chevaliers in marvellous great force;
Fifty thousand the smallest column holds.
The first is raised of men from Butenrot,
The next, after, Micenes, whose heads are gross;
Along their backs, above their spinal bones,
As they were hogs, great bristles on them grow.
The third is raised from Nubles and from Blos;
The fourth is raised from Bruns and Esclavoz;
The fifth is raised from Sorbres and from Sorz;
The sixth is raised from Ermines and from Mors;
The seventh is the men of Jericho;
Negroes are the eighth; the ninth are men of Gros;
The tenth is raised from Balide the stronghold,
That is a tribe no goodwill ever shews.
That admiral hath sworn, the way he knows,
By Mahumet, his virtues and his bones:
"Charlès of France is mad to canter so;
Battle he'll have, unless he take him home;
No more he'll wear on 's head that crown of gold."

CCXXXIII

Ten great columns they marshal thereafter:
Of Canelious, right ugly, is the first,
Who from Val-Fuit came across country there;
The next's of Turks; of Persians is the third;
The fourth is raised of desperate Pinceners,
The fifth is raised from Soltras and Avers;
The sixth is from Ormaleus and Eugez;
The seventh is the tribe of Samuel;

The eighth is from Bruise; the ninth from Esclavers;
The tenth is from Occiant, the desert,
That is a tribe, do not the Lord God serve,
Of such felons you never else have heard;
Hard is their hide, as though it iron were,
Wherefore of helm or hauberk they've no care;
In the battle they're felon murderers. AOI.

CCXXXIV

That admiral ten columns more reviews;
The first is raised of Giants from Malpruse;
The next of Huns; the third a Hungar crew;
And from Baldise the Long the fourth have trooped;
The fifth is raised of men from Val-Penuse;
The sixth is raised of tribesmen from Maruse;
The seventh is from Leus and Astrimunes;
The eighth from Argoilles; the ninth is from Clarbune;
The tenth is raised of beardsmen from Val-Frunde,
That is a tribe, no love of God e'er knew.
Gesta Francor' these thirty columns prove.
Great are the hosts, their horns come sounding through.
Pagans canter as men of valour should. AOI.

CCXXXV

That admiral hath great possessions;
He makes them bear before him his dragon,
And their standard, Tervagan's and Mahom's,
And his image, Apollin the felon.
Ten Canelious canter in the environs,
And very loud they cry out this sermon:
"Let who would from our gods have garrison,
Serve them and pray with great affliction."
Pagans awhile their heads and faces on
Their breasts abase, their polished helmets doff.
And the Franks say: "Now shall you die, gluttons;

This day shall bring you vile confusion!
Give warranty, our God, unto Carlon!
And in his name this victory be won!" AOI.

CCXXXVI

That admiral hath wisdom great indeed;
His son to him and those two kings calls he:
"My lords barons, beforehand canter ye,
All my columns together shall you lead;
But of the best I'll keep beside me three:
One is of Turks; the next of Ormaleis;
And the third is the Giants of Malpreis.
And Occiant's, they'll also stay with me,
Until with Charles and with the Franks they meet.
That Emperour, if he combat with me,
Must lose his head, cut from his shoulders clean;
He may be sure naught else for him's decreed." AOI.

CCXXXVII

Great are the hosts, and all the columns fair,
No peak nor vale nor cliff between them there,
Thicket nor wood, nor ambush anywhere;
Across the plain they see each other well.
Says Baligant: "My pagan tribes adverse,
Battle to seek, canter ye now ahead!"
Carries the ensign Amboires of Oluferne;
Pagans cry out, by Preciuse they swear.
And the Franks say: "Great hurt this day you'll get!"
And very loud "Monjoie!" they cry again.
That Emperour has bid them sound trumpets;
And the olifant sounds over all its knell.
The pagans say: "Carlun's people are fair.
Battle we'll have, bitter and keenly set." AOI.

CCXXXVIII

Great is that plain, and wide is that country;

Their helmets shine with golden jewellery,
Also their sarks embroidered and their shields,
And the ensigns fixed on all their burnished spears.
The trumpets sound, their voice is very clear,
And the olifant its echoing music speaks.
Then the admiral, his brother calleth he,
'Tis Canabeus, the king of Floredee,
Who holds the land unto the Vale Sevree;
He's shewn to him Carlun's ten companies:
"The pride of France, renownèd land, you see.
That Emperour canters right haughtily,
His bearded men are with him in the rear;
Over their sarks they have thrown out their beards
Which are as white as driven snows that freeze.
Strike us they will with lances and with spears:
Battle with them we'll have, prolonged and keen;
Never has man beheld such armies meet."
Further than one might cast a rod that's peeled
Goes Baligant before his companies.
His reason then he's shewn to them, and speaks:
"Pagans, come on; for now I take the field."
His spear in hand he brandishes and wields,
Towards Carlun has turned the point of steel. AOI.

CCXXXIX

Charlès the Great, when he sees the admiral
And the dragon, his ensign and standard;—
(In such great strength are mustered those Arabs
Of that country they've covered every part
Save only that whereon the Emperour was.)
The King of France in a loud voice has called:
"Barons and Franks, good vassals are ye all,
Ye in the field have fought so great combats;
See the pagans; they're felons and cowards,

No pennyworth is there in all their laws.
Though they've great hosts, my lords, what matters that
Let him go hence, who'ld fail me in the attack."
Next with both spurs he's gored his horse's flanks,
And Tencendor has made four bounds thereat.
Then say the Franks: "This King's a good vassal.
Canter, brave lord, for none of us holds back."

CCXL

Clear is the day, and the sun radiant;
The hosts are fair, the companies are grand.
The first columns are now come hand to hand.
The count Rabel and the count Guinemans
Let fall the reins on their swift horses' backs,
Spurring in haste; then on rush all the Franks,
And go to strike, each with his trenchant lance. AOI.

CCXLI

That count Rabel, he was a hardy knight,
He pricked his horse with spurs of gold so fine,
The Persian king, Torleu, he went to strike.
Nor shield nor sark could such a blow abide;
The golden spear his carcass passed inside;
Flung down upon a little bush, he died.
Then say the Franks: "Lord God, be Thou our guide!
Charlès we must not fail; his cause is right." AOI.

CCXLII

And Guineman tilts with the king Leutice;
Has broken all the flowers on his shield,
Next of his sark he has undone the seam,
All his ensign thrust through the carcass clean,
So flings him dead, let any laugh or weep.
Upon that blow, the Franks cry out with heat:
"Strike on, baron, nor slacken in your speed!
Charle's in the right against the pagan breed;

God sent us here his justice to complete." AOI.

CCXLIII

Pure white the horse whereon Malprimès sate;
Guided his corse amid the press of Franks,
Hour in, hour out, great blows he struck them back,
And, ever, dead one upon others packed.
Before them all has cried out Baligant:
"Barons, long time I've fed you at my hand.
Ye see my son, who goes on Carlun's track,
And with his arms so many lords attacks;
Better vassal than him I'll not demand.
Go, succour him, each with his trenchant lance!"
Upon that word the pagans all advance;
Grim blows they strike, the slaughter's very grand,
And marvellous and weighty the combat:
Before nor since was never such attack. AOI.

CCXLIV

Great are the hosts; the companies in pride
Come touching, all the breadth of either side;
And the pagans do marvellously strike.
So many shafts, by God! in pieces lie
And crumpled shields, and sarks with mail untwined!
So spattered all the earth there would you find
That through the field the grass so green and fine
With men's life-blood is all vermilion dyed.
That admiral rallies once more his tribe:
"Barons, strike on, shatter the Christian line."
Now very keen and lasting is the fight,
As never was, before or since that time;
The finish none shall reach, unless he die. AOI.

CCXLV

That admiral to all his race appeals;
"Pagans, strike on; came you not therefore here?

I promise you noble women and dear,
I promise you honours and lands and fiefs."
Answer pagans: "We must do well indeed."
With mighty blows they shatter all their spears;
Five score thousand swords from their scabbards leap,
Slaughter then, grim and sorrowful, you'd seen.
Battle he saw, that stood those hosts between. AOI.

CCXLVI

That Emperour calls on his Franks and speaks:
"I love you, lords, in whom I well believe;
So many great battles you've fought for me,
Kings overthrown, and kingdoms have redeemed!
Guerdon I owe, I know it well indeed;
My lands, my wealth, my body are yours to keep.
Vengeance for sons, for heirs, for brothers wreak
Who in Rencesvals were slaughtered yestereve!
Mine is the right, ye know, gainst pagan breeds."
Answer the Franks: "Sire, 'tis the truth you speak."
Twenty thousand beside him Charlès leads,
Who with one voice have sworn him fealty;
In straits of death they never will him leave.
There is not one thenceforth employs his spear,
But with their swords they strike in company.
The battle is straitened marvellously. AOI.

CCXLVII

Across that field the bold Malprimès canters;
Who of the Franks hath wrought there much great damage.
Naimès the Duke right haughtily regards him,
And goes to strike him, like a man of valour,
And of his shield breaks all the upper margin,
Tears both the sides of his embroidered ha'berk,
Through the carcass thrusts all his yellow banner;
So dead among sev'n hundred else he casts him.

CCXLVIII

King Canabeus, brother of the admiral,
Has pricked his horse with spurs in either flank;
He's drawn his sword, whose hilt is of crystal,
And strikes Naimun on's helmet principal;
Away from it he's broken off one half,
Five of the links his brand of steel hath knapped;
No pennyworth the hood is after that;
Right to the flesh he slices through the cap;
One piece of it he's flung upon the land.
Great was the blow; the Duke, amazed thereat,
Had fallen ev'n, but aid from God he had;
His charger's neck he clasped with both his hands.
Had but the pagan once renewed the attack,
Then was he slain, that noble old vassal.
Came there to him, with succour, Charles of France.

CCXLIX AOI.

Keen anguish then he suffers, that Duke Naimès,
And the pagan, to strike him, hotly hastens.
"Culvert," says Charles, "You'll get now as you gave him!"
With vassalage he goes to strike that pagan,
Shatters his shield, against his heart he breaks it,
Tears the chin-guard above his hauberk mailèd;
So flings him dead: his saddle shall be wasted.

CCL

Bitter great grief has Charlemagne the King,
Who Duke Naimun before him sees lying,
On the green grass all his clear blood shedding.
Then the Emperour to him this counsel gives:
"Fair master Naimes, canter with me to win!
The glutton's dead, that had you straitly pinned;
Through his carcass my spear I thrust once in."
Answers the Duke: "Sire, I believe it, this.

Great proof you'll have of valour, if I live."
They 'ngage them then, true love and faith swearing;
A thousand score of Franks surround them still.
Nor is there one, but slaughters, strikes and kills. AOI.

CCLI

Then through the field cantered that admiral,
Going to strike the county Guineman;
Against his heart his argent shield he cracked,
The folds of his hauberk apart he slashed,
Two of his ribs out of his side he hacked,
So flung him dead, while still his charger ran.
After, he slew Gebuin and Lorain,
Richard the old, the lord of those Normans.
"Preciuse," cry pagans, "is valiant!
Baron, strike on; here have we our warrant!" AOI.

CCLII

Who then had seen those Arrabit chevaliers,
From Occiant, from Argoille and from Bascle!
And well they strike and slaughter with their lances;
But Franks, to escape they think it no great matter;
On either side dead men to the earth fall crashing.
Till even-tide 'tis very strong, that battle;
Barons of France do suffer much great damage,
Grief shall be there ere the two hosts be scattered.
AOI.

CCLIII

Right well they strike, both Franks and Arrabies,
Breaking the shafts of all their burnished spears.
Whoso had seen that shattering of shields,
Whoso had heard those shining hauberks creak,
And heard those shields on iron helmets beat,
Whoso had seen fall down those chevaliers,
And heard men groan, dying upon that field,

Some memory of bitter pains might keep.
That battle is most hard to endure, indeed.
And the admiral calls upon Apollin
And Tervagan and Mahum, prays and speaks:
"My lords and gods, I've done you much service;
Your images, in gold I'll fashion each:
Against Carlun give me your warranty!"
Comes before him his dear friend Gemalfin,
Evil the news he brings to him and speaks:
"Sir Baliganz, this day in shame you're steeped;
For you have lost your son, even Malprime;
And Canabeus, your brother, slain is he.
Fairly two Franks have got the victory;
That Emperour was one, as I have seen;
Great limbs he has, he's every way Marquis,
White is his beard as flowers in April."
That admiral has bent his head down deep,
And thereafter lowers his face and weeps,
Fain would he die at once, so great his grief;
He calls to him Jangleu from over sea. AOI.

CCLIV

Says the admiral: "Jangleu, beside me stand!
For you are proof, and greatly understand,
Counsel from you I've ever sought to have.
How seems it you, of Arrabits and Franks,
Shall we from hence victorious go back?"
He answers him: "Slain are you, Baligant!
For from your gods you'll never have warrant.
So proud is Charles, his men so valiant,
Never saw I a race so combatant.
But call upon barons of Occiant,
Turks and Enfruns, Arrabits and Giants.
No more delay: what must be, take in hand."

CCLV

That admiral has shaken out his beard
That ev'n so white as thorn in blossom seems;
He'll no way hide, whate'er his fate may be,
Then to his mouth he sets a trumpet clear,
And clearly sounds, so all the pagans hear.
Throughout the field rally his companies.
From Occiant, those men who bray and bleat,
And from Argoille, who, like dogs barking, speak;
Seek out the Franks with such a high folly,
Break through their line, the thickest press they meet
Dead from that shock they've seven thousand heaped.

CCLVI

The count Oger no cowardice e'er knew,
Better vassal hath not his sark indued.
He sees the Franks, their columns broken through,
So calls to him Duke Tierris, of Argune,
Count Jozeran, and Gefreid, of Anjou;
And to Carlun most proud his reason proves:
"Behold pagans, and how your men they slew!
Now from your head please God the crown remove
Unless you strike, and vengeance on them do!"
And not one word to answer him he knew;
They spurred in haste, their horses let run loose,
And, wheresoe'er they met the pagans, strook. AOI.

CCLVII

Now very well strikes the King Charlemagne,
Naimès the Duke, also Oger the Dane,
Geifreid d'Anjou, who that ensign displays;
Exceeding proof is Don Oger, the Dane;
He spurs his horse, and lets him run in haste,
So strikes that man who the dragon displays;
Both in the field before his feet he breaks

That king's ensign and dragon, both abased.
Baligant sees his gonfalon disgraced,
And Mahumet's standard thrown from its place;
That admiral at once perceives it plain,
That he is wrong, and right is Charlemain.
Pagan Arabs coyly themselves contain;
That Emperour calls on his Franks again:
"Say, barons, come, support me, in God's Name!"
Answer the Franks: "Question you make in vain;
All felon he that dares not exploits brave!" AOI.

CCLVIII

Passes that day, turns into vesper-tide.
Franks and pagans still with their swords do strike.
Brave vassals they, who brought those hosts to fight,
Never have they forgotten their ensigns;
That admiral still "Preciuse" doth cry,
Charlès "Monjoie," renownèd word of pride.
Each the other knows by his clear voice and high;
Amid the field they're both come into sight,
Then, as they go, great blows on either side
They with their spears on their round targes strike;
And shatter them, beneath their buckles wide;
And all the folds of their hauberks divide;
But bodies, no; wound them they never might.
Broken their girths, downwards their saddles slide;
Both those Kings fall, themselves aground do find;
Nimbly enough upon their feet they rise;
Most vassal-like they draw their swords outright.
From this battle they'll ne'er be turned aside
Nor make an end, without that one man die. AOI.

CCLIX

A great vassal was Charles, of France the Douce;
That admiral no fear nor caution knew.

Those swords they had, bare from their sheaths they drew;
Many great blows on 's shield each gave and took;
The leather pierced, and doubled core of wood;
Down fell the nails, the buckles brake in two;
Still they struck on, bare in their sarks they stood.
From their bright helms the light shone forth anew.
Finish nor fail that battle never could
But one of them must in the wrong be proved. AOI.

CCLX

Says the admiral: "Nay, Charles, think, I beg,
And counsel take that t'wards me you repent!
Thou'st slain my son, I know that very well;
Most wrongfully my land thou challengest;
Become my man, a fief from me thou'lt get;
Come, serving me, from here to the Orient!"
Charle answers him: "That were most vile offence;
No peace nor love may I to pagan lend.
Receive the law that God to us presents,
Christianity, and then I'll love thee well;
Serve and believe the King Omnipotent!"
Says Baligant: "Evil sermon thou saist."
They go to strike with th' swords, are on their belts.

CCLXI AOI.

In the admiral is much great virtue found;
He strikes Carlun on his steel helm so brown,
Has broken it and rent, above his brow,
Through his thick hair the sword goes glancing round,
A great palm's breadth and more of flesh cuts out,
So that all bare the bone is, in that wound.
Charles tottereth, falls nearly to the ground;
God wills not he be slain or overpow'red.
Saint Gabriel once more to him comes down,
And questions him: "Great King, what doest thou?"

CCLXII

Charles, hearing how that holy Angel spake,
Had fear of death no longer, nor dismay;
Remembrance and a fresh vigour he's gained.
So the admiral he strikes with France's blade,
His helmet breaks, whereon the jewels blaze,
Slices his head, to scatter all his brains,
And, down unto the white beard, all his face;
So he falls dead, recovers not again.
"Monjoie," cries Charles, that all may know the tale.
Upon that word is come to him Duke Naimes,
Holds Tencendur, bids mount that King so Great.
Pagans turn back, God wills not they remain.
And Franks have all their wish, be that what may.

CCLXIII

Pagans are fled, ev'n as the Lord God wills;
Chase them the Franks, and the Emperour therewith.
Says the King then: "My Lords, avenge your ills,
Unto your hearts' content, do what you will!
For tears, this morn, I saw your eyes did spill."
Answer the Franks: "Sir, even so we will."
Then such great blows, as each may strike, he gives
That few escape, of those remain there still.

CCLXIV

Great was the heat, the dust arose and blew;
Still pagans fled, and hotly Franks pursued.
The chase endured from there to Sarraguce.
On her tower, high up clomb Bramimunde,
Around her there the clerks and canons stood
Of the false law, whom God ne'er loved nor knew;
Orders they'd none, nor were their heads tonsured.
And when she saw those Arrabits confused
Aloud she cried: "Give us your aid, Mahume!"

Ah! Noble king, conquered are all our troops,
And the admiral to shameful slaughter put!"
When Marsile heard, towards the wall he looked,
Wept from his eyes, and all his body stooped,
So died of grief. With sins he's so corrupt;
The soul of him to Hell live devils took.

CCLXV

Pagans are slain; the rest are put to rout
Whom Charlès hath in battle overpowered.
Of Sarraguce the gates he's battered down,
For well he knows there's no defence there now;
In come his men, he occupies that town;
And all that night they lie there in their pow'r.
Fierce is that King, with 's hoary beard, and proud,
And Bramimunde hath yielded up her towers;—
But ten were great, and lesser fifty around.
Great exploits his whom the Lord God endows!

CCLXVI

Passes the day, the darkness is grown deep,
But all the stars burn, and the moon shines clear.
And Sarraguce is in the Emperour's keep.
A thousand Franks he bids seek through the streets,
The synagogues and the mahumeries;
With iron malls and axes which they wield
They break the idols and all the imageries;
So there remain no fraud nor falsity.
That King fears God, and would do His service,
On water then Bishops their blessing speak,
And pagans bring into the baptistry.
If any Charles with contradiction meet
Then hanged or burned or slaughtered shall he be.
Five score thousand and more are thus redeemed,
Very Christians; save that alone the queen

To France the Douce goes in captivity:
By love the King will her conversion seek.

CCLXVII

Passes the night, the clear day opens now.
Of Sarraguce Charles garrisons the tow'rs;
A thousand knights he's left there, fighters stout,
Who guard that town as bids their Emperour.
After, the King and all his army mount,
And Bramimunde a prisoner is bound,
No harm to her, but only good he's vowed.
So are they come, with joy and gladness out,
They pass Nerbone by force and by vigour,
Come to Burdele, that city of high valour.
Above the altar, to Saint Sevrin endowed,
Stands the olifant, with golden pieces bound;
All the pilgrims may see it, who thither crowd.
Passing Girunde in great ships, there abound,
Ev'n unto Blaive he's brought his nephew down
And Oliver, his noble companioun,
And the Archbishop, who was so wise and proud.
In white coffers he bids them lay those counts
At Saint Romain: so rest they in that ground.
Franks them to God and to His Angels vow.
Charles canters on, by valleys and by mounts,
Not before Aix will he not make sojourn;
Canters so far, on th' terrace he dismounts.
When he is come into his lofty house,
By messengers he seeks his judges out;
Saxons, Baivers, Lotherencs and Frisouns,
Germans he calls, and also calls Borgounds;
From Normandy, from Brittany and Poitou,
And those in France that are the sagest found.
Thereon begins the cause of Gueneloun.

CCLXVIII

That Emperour, returning out of Spain,
Arrived in France, in his chief seat, at Aix,
Clomb to th' Palace, into the hall he came.
Was come to him there Alde, that fair dame;
Said to the King: "Where's Rollant the Captain,
Who sware to me, he'ld have me for his mate?"
Then upon Charles a heavy sorrow weighed,
And his eyes wept, he tore his beard again:
"Sister, dear friend, of a dead man you spake.
I'll give you one far better in exchange,
That is Loewis, what further can I say;
He is my son, and shall my marches take."

Alde answered him: "That word to me is strange.
Never, please God, His Angels and His Saints,
When Rollant's dead shall I alive remain!"
Her colour fails, at th' feet of Charlemain,
She falls; she's dead. Her soul God's Mercy awaits!
Barons of France weep therefore and complain.

CCLXIX

Alde the fair is gone now to her rest.
Yet the King thought she was but swooning then,
Pity he had, our Emperour, and wept,
Took her in's hands, raised her from th' earth again;
On her shoulders her head still drooped and leant.
When Charlès saw that she was truly dead
Four countesses at once he summonèd;
To a monast'ry of nuns they bare her thence,
All night their watch until the dawn they held;
Before the altar her tomb was fashioned well;
Her memory the King with honour kept. AOI.

CCLXX

That Emperour is now returned to Aix.
The felon Guene, all in his iron chains,
Is in that town, before the King's Palace;
Those serfs have bound him, fast upon his stake,
In deer-hide thongs his hands they've helpless made,
With clubs and whips they trounce him well and baste:
He has deserved not any better fate;
In bitter grief his trial there he awaits.

CCLXXI

Written it is, and in an ancient geste,
How Charlès called from many lands his men,
Assembled them at Aix, in his Chapelle.
Holy that day, for some chief feast was held,
Saint Silvester's that baron's, many tell.

Thereon began the trial and defence
Of Guenelun, who had the treason spelt.
Before himself the Emperour has him led. AOI.

CCLXXII

"Lords and barons," Charlès the King doth speak,
"Of Guenelun judge what the right may be!
He was in th' host, even in Spain with me;
There of my Franks a thousand score did steal,
And my nephew, whom never more you'll see,
And Oliver, in 's pride and courtesy,
And, wealth to gain, betrayed the dozen peers."
"Felon be I," said Guenes, "aught to conceal!
He did from me much gold and wealth forfeit,
Whence to destroy and slay him did I seek;
But treason, no; I vow there's not the least."
Answer the Franks: "Take counsel now must we."

CCLXXIII

So Guenelun, before the King there, stood;
Lusty his limbs, his face of gentle hue;
Were he loyal, right baron-like he'd looked.
He saw those Franks, and all who'ld judge his doom,
And by his side his thirty kinsmen knew.
After, he cried aloud; his voice was full:
"For th' Love of God, listen to me, baruns!
I was in th' host, beside our Emperour,
Service I did him there in faith and truth.
Hatred of me had Rollant, his nephew;
So he decreed death for me and dolour.
Message I bare to king Marsiliun;
By my cunning I held myself secure.
To that fighter Rollant my challenge threw,
To Oliver, and all their comrades too;
Charlès heard that, and his noble baruns.

Vengeance I gat, but there's no treason proved."
Answered the Franks: "Now go we to the moot."

CCLXXIV

When Guenès sees, his great cause is beginning,
Thirty he has around him of his kinsmen,
There's one of them to whom the others listen,
'Tis Pinabel, who in Sorence castle liveth;
Well can he speak, soundly his reasons giving,
A good vassal, whose arm to fight is stiffened.
Says to him Guenes: "In you my faith is fixèd.
Save me this day from death, also from prison."
Says Pinabel: "Straightway you'll be delivered.
Is there one Frank, that you to hang committeth?
Let the Emperour but once together bring us,
With my steel brand he shall be smartly chidden."
Guenès the count kneels at his feet to kiss them.

CCLXXV

To th' counsel go those of Baivere and Saxe,
Normans also, with Poitevins and Franks;
Enough there are of Tudese and Germans.
Those of Alverne the greatest court'sy have,
From Pinabel most quietly draw back.
Says each to each: "'Twere well to let it stand.
Leave we this cause, and of the King demand
That he cry quits with Guenès for this act;
With love and faith he'll serve him after that.
Since he is dead, no more ye'll see Rollant,
Nor any wealth nor gold may win him back.
Most foolish then is he, would do combat."
There is but one agrees not to their plan;
Tierri, brother to Don Geifreit, 's that man. AOI.

CCLXXVI

Then his barons, returning to Carlun,

Say to their King: "Sire, we beseech of you
That you cry quits with county Guenelun,
So he may serve you still in love and truth;
Nay let him live, so noble a man 's he proved.
Rollant is dead, no longer in our view,
Nor for no wealth may we his life renew."
Then says the King: "You're felons all of you!" AOI.

CCLXXVII

When Charlès saw that all of them did fail,
Deep down he bowed his head and all his face;
For th' grief he had, caitiff himself proclaimed.
One of his knights, Tierris, before him came,
Gefrei's brother, that Duke of Anjou famed;
Lean were his limbs, and lengthy and delicate,
Black was his hair and somewhat brown his face;
Was not too small, and yet was hardly great;
And courteously to the Emperour he spake:
"Fair Lord and King, do not yourself dismay!
You know that I have served you many ways:
By my ancestors should I this cause maintain.
And if Rollant was forfeited to Guenes,
Still your service to him full warrant gave.
Felon is Guene, since th' hour that he betrayed,
And, towards you, is perjured and ashamed:
Wherefore I judge that he be hanged and slain,
His carcass flung to th' dogs beside the way,
As a felon who felony did make.
But, has he a friend that would dispute my claim
With this my sword which I have girt in place
My judgement will I warrant every way."
Answer the Franks: "Now very well you spake."

CCLXXVIII

Before the King is now come Pinabel;

Great is he, strong, vassalous and nimble;
Who bears his blow has no more time to dwell:
Says to him: "Sire, on you this cause depends;
Command therefore this noise be made an end.
See Tierri here, who hath his judgement dealt;
I cry him false, and will the cause contest."
His deer-hide glove in the King's hand he's left.
Says the Emperour: "Good pledges must I get."
Thirty kinsmen offer their loyal pledge.
"I'll do the same for you," the King has said;
Until the right be shewn, bids guard them well. AOI.

CCLXXIX

When Tierri sees that battle shall come after,
His right-hand glove he offereth to Charlès.
That Emperour by way of hostage guards it;
Four benches then upon the place he marshals
Where sit them down champions of either party.
They're chos'n aright, as the others' judgement cast them;
Oger the Dane between them made the parley.
Next they demand their horses and their armour. AOI.

CCLXXX

For battle, now, ready you might them see,
They're well confessed, absolved, from sin set free;
Masses they've heard, Communion received,
Rich offerings to those minsters they leave.
Before Carlun now both the two appear:
They have their spurs, are fastened on their feet,
And, light and strong, their hauberks brightly gleam;
Upon their heads they've laced their helmets clear,
And girt on swords, with pure gold hilted each;
And from their necks hang down their quartered shields;
In their right hands they grasp their trenchant spears.
At last they mount on their swift coursing steeds.

Five score thousand chevaliers therefor weep,
For Rollant's sake pity for Tierri feel.
God knows full well which way the end shall be.

CCLXXXI

Down under Aix there is a pasture large
Which for the fight of th' two barons is marked.
Proof men are these, and of great vassalage,
And their horses, unwearied, gallop fast;
They spur them well, the reins aside they cast,
With virtue great, to strike each other, dart;
All of their shields shatter and rend apart.
Their hauberks tear; the girths asunder start,
The saddles slip, and fall upon the grass.
Five score thousand weep, who that sign regard. AOI.

CCLXXXII

Upon the ground are fallen both the knights;
Nimbly enough upon their feet they rise.
Nimble and strong is Pinabel, and light.
Each the other seeks; horses are out of mind,
But with those swords whose hilts with gold are lined
Upon those helms of steel they beat and strike;
Great are the blows, those helmets to divide.
The chevaliers of France do much repine.
"O God!" says Charles, "Make plain to us the right!"

CCLXXXIII

Says Pinabel: "Tierri, I pray thee, yield:
I'll be thy man, in love and fealty;
For thy pleasure my wealth I'll give to thee;
But make the King with Guenelun agree."
Answers Tierri: "Such counsel's not for me.
Pure felon I, if e'er I that concede!
God shall this day the right shew, us between!"
AOI.

CCLXXXIV

Then said Tierri: "Bold art thou, Pinabel,
Thou'rt great and strong, with body finely bred;
For vassalage thy peers esteem thee well:
Of this battle let us now make an end!
With Charlemagne I soon will have thee friends;
To Guenelun such justice shall be dealt
Day shall not dawn but men of it will tell."
"Please the Lord God, not so!" said Pinabel.
"I would sustain the cause of my kindred
No mortal man is there from whom I've fled;
Rather I'ld die than hear reproaches said."
Then with their swords began to strike again
Upon those helms that were with gold begemmed
Into the sky the bright sparks rained and fell.
It cannot be that they be sunderèd,
Nor make an end, without one man be dead. AOI.

CCLXXXV

He's very proof, Pinabel of Sorence,
Tierri he strikes, on 's helmet of Provence,
Leaps such a spark, the grass is kindled thence;
Of his steel brand the point he then presents,
On Tierri's brow the helmet has he wrenched
So down his face its broken halves descend;
And his right cheek in flowing blood is drenched;
And his hauberk, over his belly, rent.
God's his warrant, Who death from him prevents. AOI.

CCLXXXVI

Sees Tierri then that in the face he's struck,
On grassy field runs clear his flowing blood;
Strikes Pinabel on 's helmet brown and rough,
To the nose-piece he's broken it and cut,
And from his head scatters his brains in th' dust;

Brandishes him on th' sword, till dead he's flung.
Upon that blow is all the battle won.
Franks cry aloud: "God hath great virtue done.
It is proved right that Guenelun be hung
And those his kin, that in his cause are come." AOI.

CCLXXXVII

Now that Tierri the battle fairly wins,
That Emperour Charlès is come to him;
Forty barons are in his following,
Naimès the Duke, Oger that Danish Prince,
Gefrei d'Anjou, Willalme of Blaive therewith.
Tierri, the King takes in his arms to kiss;
And wipes his face with his great marten-skins;
He lays them down, and others then they bring;
The chevaliers most sweetly disarm him;
An Arab mule they've brought, whereon he sits.
With baronage and joy they bring him in.
They come to Aix, halt and dismount therein.
The punishment of the others then begins.

CCLXXXVIII

His counts and Dukes then calls to him Carlun:
"With these I guard, advise what shall be done.
Hither they came because of Guenelun;
For Pinabel, as pledges gave them up."
Answer the Franks: "Shall not of them live one."
The King commands his provost then, Basbrun:
"Go hang them all on th' tree of cursèd wood!
Nay, by this beard, whose hairs are white enough,
If one escape, to death and shame thou'rt struck!"
He answers him: "How could I act, save thus?"
With an hundred serjeants by force they come;
Thirty of them there are, that straight are hung.
Who betrays man, himself and 's friends undoes. AOI.

CCLXXXIX

Then turned away the Baivers and Germans
And Poitevins and Bretons and Normans.
Fore all the rest, 'twas voted by the Franks
That Guenès die with marvellous great pangs.
So to lead forth four stallions they bade;
After, they bound his feet and both his hands;
Those steeds were swift, and of a temper mad;
Which, by their heads, led forward four serjeants
Towards a stream that flowed amid that land.
Sonès fell Gue into perdition black;
All his sinews were strained until they snapped,
And all the limbs were from his body dragged;
On the green grass his clear blood gushed and ran.
Guenès is dead, a felon recreant.
Who betrays man, need make no boast of that.

CCXC

When the Emperour had made his whole vengeance,
He called to him the Bishops out of France,
Those of Baivere and also the Germans:
"A dame free-born lies captive in my hands,
So oft she's heard sermons and reprimands,
She would fear God, and christening demands.
Baptise her then, so God her soul may have."
They answer him: "Sponsors the rite demands,
Dames of estate and long inheritance."
The baths at Aix great companies attract;
There they baptised the Queen of Sarazands,
And found for her the name of Juliane.
Christian is she by very cognisance.

CCXCI

When the Emperour his justice hath achieved,
His mighty wrath's abated from its heat,

And Bramimunde has christening received;
Passes the day, the darkness is grown deep,
And now that King in 's vaulted chamber sleeps.
Saint Gabriel is come from God, and speaks:
"Summon the hosts, Charlès, of thine Empire,
Go thou by force into the land of Bire,
King Vivien thou'lt succour there, at Imphe,
In the city which pagans have besieged.
The Christians there implore thee and beseech."
Right loth to go, that Emperour was he:
"God!" said the King. "My life is hard indeed!"
Tears filled his eyes, he tore his snowy beard.

SO ENDS THE TALE
WHICH
TUROLD HATH CONCEIVED.

NOTE

In preparing this reprint of Scott Moncrieff's translation, I have made bold to alter slightly the punctuation, and the spelling of some proper names, for the sake of increased clarity, but always in accordance with the text of the Oxford MS as presented by Joseph Bédier. In a few instances I have also amended lines, where I felt quite certain that the translator had in some degree misread the meaning—but these instances are of minor significance.

A bibliography of the editions and critical or historical literature of the *Song of Roland* would be out of place in these pages. But readers who may wish to explore the poem and its significance for themselves may be advised to start with:

I. the cheap and readily accessible edition of Léon Gautier, reprinted in numerous editions since its first appearance in 1872;

II. the two-volume edition of Joseph Bédier, 1924;

III. Léon Gautier's *Les Épopées Françaises*;

IV. *Histoire Poëtique de Charlemagne*, and *Légendes du Moyen Âge*, both by Gaston Paris.

H. M.

For this edition C. K. Scott Moncrieff's rendering of The Song of Roland has been edited by Hamish Miles. Fifteen hundred copies have been printed for the members of The Limited Editions Club by Edmund B. Thompson at Hawthorn House, Windham, Connecticut. The illustrations have been made by Valenti Angelo; each copy has been illuminated by Mr. Angelo whose signature is placed

Valenti Angelo

upon this copy, number

1335